$20.

D0516357

Beggars, Beasts & Easter Fire

Beggars, Beasts & Easter Fire

CAROL GREENE

ILLUSTRATIONS BY

KIMBERLY BULCKEN ROOT

Text copyright © 1993 Carol Greene
Illustrations copyright © 1993 Kimberly Bulcken Root

Published by
Lion Publishing
1705 Hubbard Avenue, Batavia, Illinois 60510, USA
ISBN 0 7459 2221 X
Lion Publishing plc
Sandy Lane West, Oxford, England
ISBN 0 7459 2221 X
Albatross Books Pty Ltd
PO Box 320, Sutherland, NSW 2232, Australia
ISBN 0 7324 0639 0

First edition 1993

Library of Congress Cataloging-in-Publication Data

Greene, Carol
      Beggars, beasts, and Easter fire : a book of early saints and heroes /
Carol Greene : illustrations by Kimberly Bulcken Root. — 1st ed.
           p. cm.
      Summary: Describes the accomplishments and struggles of twenty
important saints who lived in fourteen countries during the first fifteen
centuries of Christian history.
      ISBN 0 7459 2221 X
      1. Christian saints—Biography—Juvenile literature. [1. Saints.]
I. Root, Kimberly Bulcken, ill. II. Title.
BX4658.G74 1993
270'.092'2—dc20
      [B]   92-31408

A catalogue record for this book is available from the British Library

Printed and bound in USA

Contents

The Story of Saints

Have you ever heard someone say: "She's an absolute saint"? Has your mother ever asked you to "Be a saint and do this for me"? Have you heard an adult talk about a "sainted grandfather" who died years ago? When people use the term "saint" today, they often mean someone who is especially good or kind or patient or loving—or someone who has died. But where does the term come from? And what does it really mean?

The earliest meaning of *saint* probably comes from the Bible. Here a saint is anyone who loves and serves God, or who believes that Jesus Christ is the Son of God. But through the years, the word came to mean something more.

From time to time, there are men and women who dare to do things for their faith that more timid folk wouldn't dream of doing. These courageous people become heroes in the eyes of others. And the church recognizes them by calling them "Saints"—with a capital "S."

The first such saints were people who lived at the time of Jesus and recorded his story in the Bible. After Jesus died, rose from the dead, and ascended into heaven, his followers—the early Christian church—began to grow.

By the Middle Ages, the Christian church had become large and powerful. It gained vast areas of land and enormous political power. Its missionaries spread the story of Jesus throughout the world. Nuns and monks in the church's convents and monasteries (places where unmarried women and men dedicated their lives to the service of God) educated children and looked after poor and sick people.

Many Christians who lived during these early years became known as saints. Some were martyrs, men and women who were killed because they refused to give up their faith in Jesus. Other saints *lived* their faith heroically.

Some of these heroes faced physical danger, such as Boniface in the wild northern lands of Germany, and Joan, who battled enemy soldiers in France. Others saints, such as Margaret and Cuthbert, showed their heroism in the steady goodness of their daily lives, loving when it was hard to love and bringing joy to people everyone else had forgotten.

None of the saints was perfect. They were human, just as we are. And they often found themselves on the wrong end in the struggle between right and wrong. Francis, for instance, was wrong to steal his father's cloth in order to raise money for a church. Teresa was wrong to run away from home as a child.

But because of their brave efforts to serve God, to overcome wrong, and to help others, the church decided to give them the title of *saints.*

Through the years, the church set up a complicated system for determining who could be an official saint. This system, called canonization, involves a long and detailed study of each candidate's life. Canonization doesn't *make* a person a saint. It simply recognizes that the person *was* a saint.

Of course, many real saints never got canonized. Their lives were so quiet, so hidden that the church didn't know about them. Someone from your family or your community may be that sort of unknown saint. To remember them, the church has set aside November 1—All Saints Day—as a time to celebrate the "hidden saints."

One more thing: as stories of the saints were told again and again, legends often developed. These legends may say more about people's feelings toward the saints than about events that really happened. In their own way, though, legends can help us understand the truth about the saints and about the people whose lives were touched by these heroes.

Nicholas

Nicholas, bishop of Myra. Saint Nicholas. Sanct Herr Nicholaas. Sintirklass. Santa Claus. That, more or less, is how one name can change over some 1,500 years. The person to whom that name belonged changed too: from a tall, dignified churchman, clad in the red robe of a bishop, to a jolly old elf with a jiggly belly and a red suit trimmed with white fur. Furthermore, the bishop, who rode a fine white horse, hundreds of years later found himself packed into a sleigh along with sacks of toys. Nine flying reindeer pulled the sleigh across the sky—and one of them had the most astonishing red nose.

he story of St. Nicholas is a story about stories, a tale of legends—some old, some not so old. Behind these stories lie very few facts, but a great many feelings.

The first story, the true one, goes like this: Nicholas was a fourth-century bishop in Myra, a city in what is today Turkey. And that is all we know about his life.

After Nicholas's death, his body was buried at Myra, and soon the other stories began. Some said he had been the only son of rich parents. Others said that on the day of his birth, while his nurse was bathing him, he stood up straight on his newborn legs, folded his newborn hands, and stared into heaven.

When his parents died, says one legend, Nicholas inherited their fortune and had a wonderful time giving it away. One occasion of his gift-giving so captured people's hearts and imaginations that it has been retold in countless versions.

In the city of Patara there lived a poor man who had three daughters, all old enough to get married. But their father could not afford to give them dowries, and without a dowry—money given by a bride's father to her new husband—a girl's chances of marrying were slim.

"What shall I do?" cried the man one evening when he was feeling especially low.

"Fear not, father," replied his daughters. "Somehow, everything will turn out all right." And, good girls that they were, they washed their stockings, hung them by the fire to dry, and went to bed.

Nicholas had heard about this family and their troubles, and that very night he crept up onto their roof and tossed three bags of gold down their chimney. The bags just happened to fall into the stockings hanging by the fire, and the girls were able to marry and live happily ever after.

No doubt it was this legend that led to the story of Santa Claus getting in and out of houses through the chimney. It also gave St. Nicholas his symbol—three sacks of gold, which are now represented by the three gold balls we sometimes see outside pawnshops.

Other stories were also told of the saint, and, by the

ninth century, he had become extremely popular in many Eastern churches.

Then—and this is fact—in May, 1087, forty-seven Italians swooped down on four monks at the church in Myra and carried off the remains of St. Nicholas to Italy, where they rest to this day in the town of Bari. The saint's new resting place attracted streams of visitors from western Europe, and this started up a whole new series of legends and beliefs.

Once, on his way to the Holy Land, Nicholas supposedly calmed a stormy sea. Because of that story, he was believed to protect sailors, fishermen, and merchants. For more mysterious reasons, he was also said to protect lost husbands and college students who were having trouble with their grades. But above all, Nicholas became known as the patron saint of children.

Various lands already had assorted legends about creatures who distribute gifts to children, often around the time of Christmas. In Italy, Befana did the job. She was an old woman who climbed down chimneys and left either gifts and sweets or lumps of coal—depending on the child's behavior. In other places, children waited for Knecht Ruprecht, a grubby heathen fellow who was sometimes naughty and sometimes nice.

But the church felt strongly that one of its own saints should take over the duties of rewarding good children with gifts. "Why not St. Nicholas?" some people said. "After all, he made a fine start with those poor girls in Patara."

So little children in the Netherlands began to leave their

wooden shoes by the fireplace, along with some hay for the saint's horse. They did this on December 6, the traditional feast day of St. Nicholas. And, sure enough, on the next morning the hay was gone and the shoes brimmed over with goodies.

"Hurrah for Sinterklass!" cried the children.

Children in other lands received their Christmas gifts from St. Nicholas in other ways, but the feelings about the event were the same everywhere. It took a while, though, for St. Nicholas to cross the Atlantic and visit American children. According to one author, he finally made it to New Amsterdam by 1809, clambering down chimneys and filling stockings. But St. Nicholas still looked like a bishop in those days.

Then along came a poem that would change Nicholas forever. Its original title was "An Account of a Visit from St. Nicholas," but most people know it as "The Night Before Christmas." Some say Clement Clarke Moore, a rather stodgy professor of biblical studies, wrote the poem. Others say no, it belongs to the much livelier Henry Livingstone, Jr. The famous cartoonist Thomas Nast drew the pictures for it—and his idea of Santa Claus has been with us ever since.

Overnight the stately bishop became an elf, just big enough to hold children on his lap. His features changed too, into twinkly eyes, merry dimples, rosy cheeks, a red nose, a droll mouth, and that round, jelly-like belly. Furthermore, Nicholas's faithful white horse vanished, replaced by eight tiny reindeer—who could fly. And, if one

NICHOLAS

believed the poem, gifts must be delivered on Christmas Eve instead of on December 6.

The poem spread like an epidemic throughout the United States and across the ocean. The name Santa Claus caught on, and folk believed that every child deserved a visit from the kind old man. Even songs got into the act.

What was probably the most popular song started as a story—an advertising giveaway—in 1939. Robert L. May dreamed up a ninth reindeer, Rudolph, whose bright red nose made the other reindeer laugh at him, until a foggy night when he alone could guide Santa's sleigh. Ten years later, the story became a song, and Rudolph found his own place in legend.

Are all these legends bad? Maybe—if they cause people to forget what really happened on the first Christmas. But we can enjoy legends as long as we save our deepest joy for the real birth of God's Son.

And it might be nice if we even spared an occasional thought for the real St. Nicholas, that factual fourth-century bishop of Myra.

Augustine of Hippo

In the middle of the fourth century, the vast Roman Empire still stretched across much of Europe and even into North Africa. Beautifully built roads and palaces, marketplaces, arenas, and civic buildings marked the presence of one of the most far-flung civilizations the world has ever known. But by the year 350, cracks were appearing in the structure of the Roman Empire. Immorality and a frantic search for pleasure were fast becoming a way of life, especially for the rich and powerful. Meanwhile, Goths, Vandals, and other potential invaders looked longingly at the empire's rich lands and waited to pounce.

ugustine was born in 354 to Monica, a devout Christian woman, and her husband Patricius, a non-Christian Roman citizen. The family made its home in the village of Tagaste, Numidia, in North Africa (Souk-Ahras, Algeria, today). They did not have much money, but they managed to live a fairly comfortable life.

Augustine wrote later that he did bad things even as a baby. When the adults around him wouldn't give him what he wanted—such as sunbeams or flames from the fireplace—he'd punish them with shrieks and wails. When he was old enough to go to school, he used every lie and trick he could think of to get out of doing his lessons. At fifteen, Augustine began to steal, "not to enjoy what I stole, but because I joyed in the theft and sin itself." He especially remembered stealing huge baskets of pears from a tree near his home with some of his friends. They'd take just a bite or two of the pears, then throw the rest away.

All this while, Augustine's mother, Monica, was praying for both her husband and her son. She wanted them to find the strength and joy in Christianity that she had found. Finally, at least some of her prayers were answered: Patricius became a Christian.

Meanwhile Augustine went from bad to worse. When he was sixteen, he journeyed to the North African city of Carthage to study speaking and writing. He planned to become a lawyer, but spent much of his time at chariot races or the theatre. By the time he was eighteen, he was living with a woman who was not his wife, and they had a son, Adeodatus.

After a while, his interests led him to study philosophy and a religion called Manicheism, a mixture of Christian and pagan thought. Eventually, he rejected them both and set out on a teaching career. First in Rome and then in Milan, Augustine taught speaking and writing. By this time his father had died, and his mother came to live with Augustine in Milan. Meanwhile, Adeodatus' mother had returned to Africa, leaving the boy with his father.

In Milan, Augustine met Ambrose, a bishop and a fine preacher. He went to church just to hear Ambrose speak. And soon the words began to seep into his heart.

One day an African friend named Pontitian visited Augustine. Pontitian was excited about a Christian saint named Antony. He told Augustine how two men had converted to Christianity after they read the story of St. Antony's life. Then Pontitian began to tell that story to Augustine. As he listened, Augustine felt very strange. He already knew that part of him wanted to serve God, but part still enjoyed doing wicked things. Now the moment had come when he could no longer stand being torn in two.

As soon as Pontitian left, Augustine began to weep. He went out into his garden and threw himself down under a fig tree. Then, above the noise of his own sobs, he heard what seemed to be a child singing in a nearby house.

"Take up and read," sang the child. "Take up and read."

Convinced that God had chosen this way to speak to him, Augustine hurried back into the house, opened his Bible, and read from St. Paul's letter to the Christians in Rome: "No wild parties or drunkenness, no quarrels or jealousies! Let Jesus Christ himself be the shield that you wear; give no more thought to satisfying evil desires."

"Instantly," said Augustine later, "all the darkness of my doubt vanished." He knew that now his heart belonged to Jesus alone, and he vowed to spend all the rest of his life serving God.

Monica was overjoyed. Soon she, Augustine, Adeodatus, and other friends moved to a house in the country, where they lived as a religious community. On Easter Eve in 387, Bishop Ambrose himself baptized Augustine and his son, Adeodatus, and their friends.

Soon after that, Adeodatus died and Augustine decided to go back to Africa. Monica intended to go with him, but she also died while they were still in Italy. So Augustine returned to Tagaste without any family. There, in his childhood home, he spent three years reading, praying, and writing.

But the church needed Augustine too much to let him stay in Tagaste. In 391, he was ordained a priest. In 395, he became bishop of Hippo, a city not far from Tagaste. As bishop, one of his main jobs was watching out for groups that tried to change Christian beliefs from what Jesus originally taught. One such group was the Manicheans— whose ideas had once tempted Augustine himself.

In sermons and in writing, Augustine carefully showed how these groups were wrong. He preached every Sunday and wrote so much that it sometimes took three secretaries to keep up with him. Two of his books are still read by many people today.

The *Confessions* tells about Augustine's own life and his decision to serve God. In this book, he makes it very clear how wicked he was and how sorry he later felt about all the evil he had done.

Augustine's other great book, The *City of God*, discusses history from a Christian point of view. Many empires have come and gone, he wrote, because they were based on greedy people conquering other people. But the church— the City of God—will last forever, because it is based on God's love. These ideas and others in the book have influenced the church's teaching for over a thousand years.

Augustine himself could see the Roman Empire crumbling around him. In 410 the Goths invaded Italy and took over the city of Rome. In 430, hordes of Vandals surrounded Hippo and besieged the city. Augustine could have escaped, but he chose to stay with his people.

In any case, he did not live to see the end of the siege, which lasted fourteen months. After only three months, on August 28, 430, Augustine died peacefully from a fever at the age of seventy-six.

St. Augustine was named one of the great Doctors of the Church, because of his important teachings and writings. But a simple prayer that he wrote at the beginning of his *Confessions* may provide the best summary of his own life.

"You made us for yourself, O God, and our hearts are restless until they rest in you."

Patrick of Ireland

Not one city stood in fifth-century Ireland, not even one town or one tiny village. The whole land was countryside or forest, mile after rolling green mile. People lived on isolated plots of land called holdings. No one king ruled all of Ireland at that time. No common set of laws governed the people's actions either—only unwritten traditions passed from one generation to the next.

Wild and lonely as their lives might have been, the Irish people had treasures they could call their own. One was a deep love for nature and all its creatures. At the same time, the Irish people loved learning, and they had schools in which their children could study. Ireland had some churches too, in which Irish Christians worshipped God in their own way.

o many stories and legends have grown up around St. Patrick that it is almost impossible to dig out facts about the real person. We do know that he was born around 387 in either Scotland or Wales. His father, a Roman named Calpurnius, was a deacon in the Christian church, and his grandfather was a Christian priest. From all accounts, Patrick went to school but did not care much about learning his lessons.

When he was sixteen, a band of Irish raiders carried him off to Ireland and sold him as a slave to a chieftain in the western part of the land. There Patrick became a shepherd.

As he spent long, lonely days in the forests or hills with his sheep, his love of God grew stronger, and his faith increased.

Six years after his capture, Patrick had a dream in which a voice said to him, "Your ship is ready."

He got up immediately and trudged all the way to the southeast coast of Ireland where he did indeed find a ship ready to sail. Although he had no money to pay for his passage, the kindhearted sailors took him aboard anyway and off they went.

It's not clear where that voyage took Patrick. Some say to Gaul, some to Britain, and others place him in Rome. Wherever he ended up, Patrick became much more serious about studying. Eventually he was ordained as a deacon, then a priest, and finally a bishop in the church.

Yet, even in his new life in this distant land, Patrick could not forget Ireland. Voices of the people he had once lived with called out to him in his dreams. "We beg you, holy boy," they cried, "to come and walk among us once more."

"Thanks be to God," wrote Patrick later, "that after many years the Lord answered their cry."

In 432, Bishop Patrick set out for Ireland as a missionary. The fact that he already spoke the people's language helped him tremendously, as did his respect for the Irish culture.

Patrick loved nature just as much as the Irish people did, and sometimes he used it to explain important things about God to them.

"I don't understand the meaning of the Trinity," someone once said to him. "You talk about three persons—

Father, Son, and Holy Spirit. Yet you say they are one God. How can that be?"

Patrick bent down and picked a shamrock. "This is one plant with one stem," he said. "But it has three leaves. The Trinity is a little like this shamrock."

Of course Patrick did not approve of people worshipping nature. He once told two Irish girls: "Our God is the God of all—the God of heaven and earth, of sea and river, of sun and moon and stars, of the lofty mountain and the lowly valley." It was the God of creation—not creation itself—who was worthy of worship.

Soon after he arrived in Ireland, Patrick decided to show that God is God of all in a very dramatic way. That year a nature worshippers' festival fell on the night before Easter. Their custom was to put out all their hearth fires so that the land was utterly dark. Then they received new fire from the hearth of the local chieftain.

Patrick and other Christians travelling with him went to an area ruled by an especially powerful chieftain, King Laoghire, and climbed the hill across from the king's home at Tara. There, on Easter Eve, after the nature worshippers had put out their fires and everything was dark and still, the Christians lit the great Paschal or Easter fire.

The nature worshippers' priests, called druids, were startled and horrified.

"You must destroy that fire and the man who started it," they told King Laoghire. "Otherwise it will burn in Ireland forever."

So Laoghire sent warriors with the druids up the hill.

But, according to legend, no matter how much water and sand they used, the Easter fire kept burning. Furthermore, Patrick and his friends seemed totally unafraid. They knelt around the fire and sang songs to God.

This greatly impressed King Laoghire, who insisted on meeting Patrick the next morning. Some say it was on his way to this meeting that Patrick sang his great hymn, known as *Breastplate, Lorica,* or *Deer's Cry*:

> *I bind unto myself the Name,*
> *the strong Name of the Trinity,*
> *by invocation of the same,*
> *the Three in One, and One in Three*
> *of whom all nature hath creation,*
> *eternal Father, Spirit, Word:*
> *praise to the Lord of my salvation,*
> *salvation is of Christ the Lord.*

Laoghire did not become a Christian, but many other people did. In fact, for almost thirty years, Patrick worked in Ireland, starting churches, monasteries, convents, and schools. Nothing—not hunger, homelessness or bad weather—could stop him. As a result, some say that Patrick single-handedly converted Ireland. But Patrick himself said, "I owe it to God's grace that so many people should through me become Christians."

God certainly picked the right man for the job. The Irish people loved the way Patrick let them remain close to nature and use it to worship God. They loved the way he gave them new places for learning and the arts in the convents and monasteries he founded. But most of all they loved Patrick, and perhaps that is why they have told so many legends about him.

One of the most popular of these legends claims that Patrick drove all of the snakes out of Ireland—and, in a symbolic way, he did. He got rid of the bad parts of the people's beliefs and left them the good parts for their worship of God.

The facts of Patrick's death are unclear. Some say he returned to Britain and died at Glastonbury. Others say he died at Saul on Strangford Lough in Ireland, where he built his first church. He died between 461 and 466.

Patrick soon became known as the patron saint of Ireland, although each March 17, his feast day, many people from other countries claim him as well. Those long-ago druids were absolutely right. The fire that Patrick lit on Easter Eve still burns in Ireland—and around the world.

Columba

The monasteries founded by Patrick and his successors in Ireland fit as naturally into their surroundings as an Irish farm. Simple wooden buildings with thatched roofs sheltered the monks and the livestock they tended. Cultivated fields stretched green and golden to the surrounding woodlands.

But more than farming went on in those monasteries. Some monks made copies of the Bible, glorious manuscripts done with a quill pen and illuminated in red, blue, and gold. Other monks taught courses in monastery schools: Latin, Greek, mathematics, geometry, astronomy, music and, of course, religion. In some ways, each Irish monastery was a little world in itself. But each also held tightly to the tradition Patrick had left behind—the Celtic tradition of using nature and learning as twin tools for the worship of God.

Columba was born in 521 in Donegal on the northwest coast of Ireland. Both of his parents were of royal blood, and many people believed he could become a high king of Ireland if he wanted to. "Just look at him!" they said. "He's strong and handsome, clever and brave, too."

But Columba decided to serve God in the church. His mother should not have been surprised at this choice. One legend says that an angel visited her just before Columba was born.

"Your son will blossom for heaven and lead innumerable

souls into heaven's own country," the angel told her. Perhaps that was why Columba's mother gave him the gentle name that means "dove."

As he grew older, Columba studied at several monastery schools, as well as with a poet named Gemman, Bard of Leinster. Under Gemman's instruction, Columba found out that God had given him special gifts: a poet's eyes to see beauty in the world and a poet's voice to express that beauty for others.

As soon as he was ordained a priest, Columba rushed off to fulfil one of his most burning ambitions: to found a monastery at the town of Derry, near his birthplace. That accomplished, he took up the life of a wandering preacher, teacher, and healer, managing to start some three hundred churches along the way.

Then, when Columba was forty, his whole life changed. Some stories say that he committed a sin that led to a bloody tribal war. Other stories report that he simply heard a new call from God. Whatever the case, Columba decided to leave his beloved Ireland forever. He and twelve monks climbed into coracles—round wicker boats covered with skins—and sailed away to Iona, an island off the west coast of Scotland.

Iona is a small island, about three and a half miles long. But its quiet green beauty instantly touched the poet in Columba and he wrote:

Behold Iona!
A blessing on each eye that seeth it!

He who does a good for others here
Will find his own redoubled many-fold!

He and the others began at once to build a monastery, complete with a church and a guest house. They planted crops too. Word of their work spread, and others joined them—until the community grew to over a hundred and fifty people.

But although Iona became his home, Columba often stepped into his coracle and sailed away. He had other work to do as well. One of his first journeys was to Inverness on the Scottish mainland, where King Brude of the Picts lived. The Picts were fierce people who worshipped nature gods, and Brude had no desire to meet Columba, a Christian.

"Lock the town gates!" Brude ordered his men. "I've heard that this fellow is a powerful magician. What if his magic is stronger than ours?"

Columba smiled as the gates thudded shut. Then, in his monk's robe and sandals, he simply stood outside the gates and waited. Eventually Brude saw that he was just an ordinary man.

"Let him in," ordered the king.

So Columba had a good, long talk with Brude. Not only did Brude end up liking Columba, he also believed what the monk said about Jesus. He became a Christian himself and told all his tribes to welcome this man of God and his monks.

Thus began the travels of the monks of Iona. They went all over Scotland, into the northern part of England, to other islands, and even to Iceland. And everywhere they went, they brought the good news of Jesus Christ.

Columba was wise enough to know, though, that he couldn't always be travelling. He needed to spend time alone with God and with nature. One night in his hut on Iona, after he'd knelt for hours praying about the suffering of the world, Columba fell asleep on the stone that served as his bed. When he woke up, he saw a small robin sitting in the window.

"Do you have a song, redbreast?" Columba asked.

Then, says legend, the robin sang him her song—a sad, sweet song about how Jesus died on the cross to bring the world back to God. That song made Columba's own love for Jesus grow even greater, and he quickly called his monks together for a worship service.

"Come, too, you birds!" he cried. And from every direction came all kinds of birds. When Columba wished them the peace of God, they replied, "Peace!" After the service was over, everyone left except the robin, who sang her song again.

"Peace in the name of the Trinity," Columba said to her.

"Peace in the name of Christ," she sang back.

Many other tales have been told about Columba's love for the birds and beasts, but one of the most famous is about a white horse. Columba was an old man then, and knew that he soon would die. He looked forward to being with his Lord forever, but there were many on earth who were not ready to let him go.

One day, he had been out walking on Iona and stopped

to rest by the side of the road. Along came a white horse, who carried milk pails between the pasture and the monastery. When the horse saw Columba, he stopped, leaned his head against the old man's chest, and began to weep.

"Here! I'll take him away," said the herdsman who walked with the horse.

"Let him alone," said Columba. "He loves me. God told him that I am about to die, and he is grieving for me." Then he blessed the horse.

A few hours later, Columba did die, his face shining with joy. His last words to his monks were, "Be at peace with each other. Be kind and love one another."

That was in 597. Columba is still a much-loved saint in Scotland and Ireland.

Cuthbert of Lindisfarne

During the course of the seventh century, the ancient shadows of ignorance and superstition that had darkened the English kingdom of Northumbria at last began to flee. When good King Oswald took the throne, he brought Aidan, a saintly monk from Iona, to fan the flickering flames of Christianity lit by earlier missionaries. Aidan did more, too. On the tiny island of Lindisfarne, he founded a monastery that became a beacon of God's love to the western world.

round the year 634, a boy called Cuthbert was born in Northumbria. The identity of his parents remains a mystery, but he was raised by a kind widow whom he loved so much that he called her "Mother."

Cuthbert was a strong, athletic boy who was very good at games. One day, when he was about eight, he and some other boys were performing acrobatic tricks to see who was the best. Suddenly a three-year-old stomped up and stood in front of Cuthbert.

"Stop playing games!" he ordered. "You should be

at home studying."

After one astonished look, Cuthbert ignored him.

"You listen to me!" persisted the little boy. "God wants you to teach other people someday. You should be getting ready right now."

This time Cuthbert did listen, and he thought about what the little boy had said for a long, long time.

Some years later, young Cuthbert stood on the slope of a Northumbrian hill, watching over the sheep he was paid to guard. It was night, and around him everything else—birds, sheep, and shepherds—slept. But Cuthbert stared into the black velvet sky and thought about God. Perhaps the words of that bossy three-year-old also echoed through his mind.

All at once, a beam of light pierced the darkness and streamed to earth like a glowing pathway. Strange and brilliant spirits came down that pathway and took from the earth another spirit that burned as brightly as they. Then back they all climbed and, in an instant, the sky stretched black and still once more.

Later Cuthbert learned that Bishop Aidan of Lindisfarne had died that night. The moment he heard this news, he returned his sheep to their owner, found a horse, and set off for a monastery at the town of Melrose. The vision he had seen on that darkened hill had been a sign from God, Cuthbert decided. Now it was time to follow God's calling.

At Melrose, Cuthbert studied with the gentle and wise prior who helped to run the monastery. Eventually, he took vows as a priest. When the prior died, Cuthbert took his place at the monastery. He had always been a leader, and his skills did not fail him now.

But Cuthbert couldn't bear to spend all of his time inside the monastery. Often, he strode through the countryside, visiting lonely cottages and forgotten villages and telling the people he met the good news about Jesus Christ. Some say that he did more on these trips—that he also healed the sick and even raised the dead. Certainly his own radiant joy in God and in life was like a candle that kindled a similar joy in everyone he met.

Cuthbert, though, could never be satisfied until he felt that he'd given God all he possibly could. One story tells of the time he spent a day teaching monks and nuns at the town of Coldingham. "It is not enough," thought Cuthbert as the day ended. "I will give God my night as well."

So he slipped out of the monastery and went down by the sea to pray. One of the monks followed him, to see just what Cuthbert would do. To the monk's amazement, Cuthbert walked down into the water until the sea reached his chest. He stood there till dawn, singing praises to God.

As morning light streaked the sky and the tide ebbed, Cuthbert knelt down on the shore, still praising God. Out of the waves tumbled two little sea otters. They warmed Cuthbert's feet with their breath and dried them with their sleek fur. Then Cuthbert blessed them and the otters tumbled back into the waves.

Later in his life Cuthbert was asked to lead the monastery at Lindisfarne, the one Aidan had founded. There a hard job awaited him. But there, too, Cuthbert's patience and gentleness—and, above all, the goodness that seemed to shine from his face—won everyone over.

Finally Cuthbert decided that he must devote all his time to God alone. So he asked permission to leave Lindisfarne and live as a hermit on the lonely island of Farne. There he dug a two-room shelter out of the ground, his only window facing toward the sky. With a reluctant sigh or two, he also built a small guest house for the monks who insisted on visiting him.

But Farne, Cuthbert soon learned, wasn't nearly as lonely as he'd hoped it would be: plenty of birds lived there, too. Bold as could be, they ate up the crops he planted and stole straw from the guest-house roof to build their nests. Cuthbert lost his temper.

"You pests get out of here—now!" he shouted.

The birds fluttered away in fright. But later they crept back, obviously sorry for what they had done. So Cuthbert forgave them, and from then on they all lived together peacefully.

The day came when Cuthbert had visitors that he couldn't shoo away: a bishop, the king of Northumbria, and a number of other important people.

"We want you to be bishop of Lindisfarne," they announced. As much as Cuthbert hated the idea of leaving his island, he felt it was what God wanted him to do.

After two years at Lindisfarne, Cuthbert felt his body failing him. He again asked permission to retreat to Farne. There, after only two months, he became gravely ill. By the time monks arrived to help him, Cuthbert was near death.

He revived long enough to send messages to various

people and to receive Holy Communion for the last time. Then, lifting his hands in prayer, Cuthbert died. As his bright spirit returned to God that night in 687, one of his monks sent the news to Lindisfarne with a special sign: fiery torches against the black sky.

Boniface of Crediton

The Christian church had been alive and well in Roman Britain for almost three hundred years when Anglo-Saxon invaders stormed the land. Mercilessly they destroyed everything in their path—churches, cities, and any people who didn't flee to the north or west. By the end of the sixth century, though, Pope Gregory the Great had sent missionaries, "armed with the strength of God," to reclaim that part of Britain. They did so with amazing swiftness. Monasteries sprang up and became places of great culture. Before long, some of their monks were ready to repay Pope Gregory by going as missionaries themselves to the lands of northern Europe.

infrid—who was later to be called Boniface— was probably born at Crediton in southwest England around 680. At the age of five, he announced that he wanted to be a monk when he grew up. His parents approved. When he was seven, they sent him to school at a Benedictine monastery near Exeter. When he was fourteen, he went to another Benedictine monastery at Nursling.

Everyone liked Winfrid and admired him for his keen mind. The moment he finished his own studies, he became director of his school and began to teach others. His love for learning and his concern for his students made him a good teacher. For example, when his students had trouble learning Latin, Winfrid solved the problem by writing a better textbook for them.

When he was thirty, Winfrid became a priest in the Benedictine order, much to the delight of the other monks, who hoped to keep him at Nursling forever. But Winfrid had other ideas. In 718, he went to Rome to ask Pope Gregory II's permission to preach to the heathen lands. Gregory happily encouraged him to preach to any heathen he wanted, and he changed Winfrid's name to Boniface. Boniface then set off across the Alps and into the dark forest lands of Germany.

Not everyone in Germany was a heathen. Some missionaries had been to this area before. But over the years, Christian teaching became confused, so that Jesus sometimes seemed to be no more than the people's old war god with a different name. Their churches were badly organized and poor as well.

So Boniface found himself with two jobs: to clean up the mess that was already there and to preach about Jesus to those who had not yet heard. He'd barely started, though, when he got the chance to go to Friesland, near Holland, and work with a great missionary named Willibrord. Boniface worked with Willibrord for three exciting and success-filled years. Then he headed back to Germany, where he was also very successful. In 722 the pope recognized his achievements and asked him to come to Rome, where Boniface was made bishop of Germany.

Back in the dark forests again, Boniface decided that it was time he did something dramatic to show the people that the Christian God was the only God.

"Come to the great Oak of Thor tomorrow," he told the people in a small German village, "and you will see something worth seeing."

The next day, everyone in the village, from the oldest granny to the tiniest child, gathered around that huge, ancient tree. Of course they knew it well. It was the sacred shrine of Thor—one of their highest gods—and it played an important part in their pagan worship.

Boniface looked at the tree, from its gnarled roots to its wind-tossed branches.

"Thor is no god," he said. "If he were, he would be able to stop me from what I am about to do. Now, stand back."

Boniface picked up an axe, drew back his arms, and dealt the oak a mighty blow. Whack! That was all it took. The tree shivered and, with a thunderous crash, fell to the ground where it lay in four pieces. Because Thor did not respond, the people at once turned to God.

"Thereupon," said a follower of Boniface, "the holy bishop built a church from the timber of that oak and dedicated it to St. Peter."

After that, Boniface journeyed from place to place, building churches and monasteries as he went. So many people flocked to them that he ran short of monks and teachers. He had to write letter after letter to his friends in England, asking them to send more—and still more— people. He also needed more copies of the Bible. "Take pity," he wrote, "upon an old man worn out by troubles in this German land. Support me by your prayers to God, and help me by sending me the Sacred Writings."

In spite of his successes, Boniface must have lived a hard life. He once said, "The church is like a great ship being pounded by the waves of life's different stresses. Our duty is not to abandon ship, but to keep her on her course."

One of the things that endeared Boniface to so many was that he never got so wrapped up in his daily work that he forgot people. When he came upon a blanket woven from goat hair, he thought of the Abbot of Wearmouth and sent it to him as a present. He sent two little kegs of wine to the Archbishop of York and told him to use them "for a day of rejoicing with your friends." When a young slave couldn't get permission to marry the girl he loved, it was Boniface who spoke to the slave's owner and worked things out.

In 731, Pope Gregory III made Boniface an archbishop, and his work eventually extended all the way into northern France as well.

At last, Boniface began to feel his age. His huge flock needed a younger shepherd, he thought. He chose one of his followers, Lull, for the job. Not that Boniface himself had any intention of sitting back and putting his feet up. No, there was still work to be done with the Frieslanders in Holland. After his friend Willibrord died, many of them had slipped back into their old ways and needed to be converted all over again.

So, at the age of seventy-three, Boniface, accompanied by some of his followers, returned to Friesland. Once again, they enjoyed great success, and many people became Christians. Boniface planned to hold a huge confirmation service—a special ceremony to welcome new Christians— one spring evening. Those to be confirmed were to gather in white robes in an open field near a little river. As he waited for them to arrive, Boniface sat in his tent and read.

Suddenly a mob of fierce warriors swept down on the missionaries. Some of the missionaries were ready to fight back, but Boniface wouldn't let them.

"Children, let us not return evil for evil!" he called. A moment later, he fell dead, his head split by a sword.

Boniface was seventy-four when he died in 754 and all Europe mourned him. Archbishop Cuthbert of Canterbury said, "We in England lovingly count Boniface among the best and greatest teachers of the faith." St. Boniface remains the patron saint of Germany to this day.

Margaret of Scotland

By the middle of the eleventh century, wild, beautiful Scotland had lived through a great deal of bloody history. In 844, the country was plunged into war with the Angles and Norsemen. Later, King Duncan was foully murdered by Macbeth (according to Shakespeare's tale). Macbeth, in turn, was killed by Duncan's son, who took the throne as Malcolm III.

Meanwhile, to the south, England was going through troubles of its own. The Danish king, Canute II, had invaded the land. Because of the danger, England's king sent his young son, Edward, to safety in Hungary.

There Edward grew up and married Agatha, niece of Hungary's queen. They had three children, Christina, Margaret, and Edgar.

 e know nothing about Margaret's childhood in Hungary, except that she was born around 1045. When she was nine, King Canute II died, and her great-uncle, Edward the Confessor, took the English throne. He invited Edward and his family to return to their homeland, so that young Edgar could become king after him.

That was the beginning of a happy chapter in Margaret's life. Although her father soon died, she and the rest of her family lived at Westminster Palace, where a kind priest became the children's teacher. Margaret loved books and learning of all kinds. Even more, she loved God and developed regular habits of prayer.

Then, in 1066, a series of events occurred that changed the course of history once again. Edward the Confessor died while Edgar, Margaret's brother, was still too young to become king. The country was left open for invasion, and William the Conqueror dashed across the sea from Normandy and seized the throne of England for himself.

According to some sources, twenty-one-year-old Margaret recognized what a danger William's presence posed for her brother. She quickly made plans to take him and Christina back to Hungary. But while their ship was still in the English Channel, a storm blew up and drove them into the North Sea. At last they limped to safety in Scotland's Firth of Forth, where warriors met their ship and marched them off to King Malcolm's castle at Edinburgh.

On the surface, Margaret seemed a gentle soul, fair and lovely to look at. But she had steel in her as well, and she must have needed every bit of it as she stood before fierce Malcolm. At least he spoke English and not only Gaelic, the sole language of many of his subjects. But what would he say to these accidental visitors to his northern kingdom?

"Welcome," was what Malcolm said. "Your great-uncle Edward once gave me a home when I had none. Now I am glad to repay him by giving one to you."

Perhaps he had already fallen in love with Margaret. It certainly wasn't long before he asked her to marry him. But at first, Margaret said no. Both she and Christina wanted to become nuns and serve God with quiet lives of prayer.

Malcolm didn't even believe in God! And, while he had many good qualities, he also loved fighting and warfare. How could Margaret serve God if she was married to someone like that?

After a time, though, Margaret came to believe that marriage to Malcolm was what God wanted for her. So the two of them exchanged vows and set up their home in Edinburgh Castle.

Before long, Malcolm noticed that his young queen disappeared for a part of each day. One day he followed her and discovered that she went to a cave near the castle. There she prayed and read from a book containing the Gospel stories about Jesus. "I don't understand anything about God," said Malcolm. "But I do know that I love you very much, Margaret. Let me turn this cave into a proper chapel for you. And—and maybe I could spend some time here with you."

So the rough king who could not read began sitting beside his wife as she read in her chapel cave. Sometimes he picked up one or another of her religious books and tenderly kissed it for love of her. Once he smuggled away her book of Gospel stories and later returned it, beautifully bound in gold and silver and studded with precious jewels. Then, finally, the day came when he knelt with Margaret and accepted the God she loved. Malcolm would always be a warrior but, from now on, Margaret would never fear for him in quite the same way.

Meanwhile, she found plenty of occasions to serve God in Scotland. When Malcolm wanted to give her a present, she asked for a monastery or a convent, an orphanage or a school. Sometimes she taught the children in these schools herself. And she asked her former teacher to send a good monk to teach the adults.

Margaret made changes at the castle, too. She taught her ladies to make beautiful tapestries and curtains to cover the cold stone walls and windows. Later they made beautiful embroideries for churches as well. Even her husband's chieftains learned table manners and how to thank God for their food before they ate it. And Margaret taught the lesson of charity, of loving and serving all of God's people.

"Poor people and sick people—and especially children—are always welcome at this castle," she decreed. "We will turn no one away."

Soon the rest of the world sat up and took notice of what was happening in Scotland.

"People there are living differently now," foreign merchants said to one another. "It might just be time to go over and offer them some of our goods." Because of the new things the merchants brought to sell, more and more Scottish people's lives became a little easier and more enjoyable.

Margaret and Malcolm had eight children, and Margaret took great care to supervise their upbringing herself. Three of the boys—Edgar, Alexander, and David—became three of Scotland's best kings. One of the girls became known as "Good Queen Maud" of England.

Toward the end of her life, Margaret's health failed and she was often in great pain. One day as she lay in her bed, holding tight to a cross, her son Edgar came into the room. He had just come from the battlefield and he brought sad news. Both King Malcolm and his eldest son had been killed by the enemy.

"I know," said Margaret in a calm voice. "God already told me of their deaths. But you, my dear Edgar, must tell me the details."

She listened quietly to her son. Then she whispered a prayer in Latin, "*Libera me.*" ("Deliver me.") With those words, Margaret of Scotland died at the age of forty-seven. She was canonized in 1250 and became patron saint of Scotland in 1673.

During her life, Margaret had worked no showy miracles, done nothing to make people point and gasp. But with the slow and steady miracle of her love—for God, for her husband, and for the people of her adopted country—she managed to change a significant part of the history of Scotland for the better.

Hildegard of Bingen

Knights on horseback and ladies in flowing gowns, rugged castles and soaring cathedrals. At first glance, twelfth-century Europe looks like a scene from a fairy tale. But this is only a small part of the picture. Behind those bright trappings lurked larger, much darker scenes. Many people, both in and out of the church, thought of nothing but money and power. Popes, princes, and a host of lesser officials plotted, schemed, and even murdered to get what they wanted. At the same time, the vast majority of people lived in unspeakable poverty, their brief lives filled with disease and suffering, while rulers of church and state pretended not to notice. At times it must have seemed as if no one remembered God. But of course many people did, and some of them spoke out against the evil around them.

ildegard was born in the summer of 1098, the tenth child of a German knight and his wife. They lived at a castle near Bingen in the rich green valley of the Rhine River in southern Germany. Green would always be important for Hildegard.

Although she was a sickly child, Hildegard was happy. But she didn't tell anyone the secret of her happiness until she was eight years old. At that time, her parents sent her to live with Jutta, a nun in a nearby Benedictine monastery. There Hildegard learned about subjects she would love for the rest of her life—music, Bible history, gardening and prayer. And there one day, she opened her heart to Jutta.

"Mother Jutta?" she began shyly. "When I was three, something happened to me. I—I had a vision from God."

"A vision?" Jutta raised her eyebrows. Was the child imagining things? "Can you tell me about it, Hildegard?"

"Well, there was a light, a—a great brightness."

"And you saw it with your own eyes?"

"N—no, not exactly. It was more as if I felt it, knew it deep inside me with—well—with my soul. Ever since then the world seems different to me. I can see God in everything he has made—plants, animals, people, everything. It's made me so happy!"

In spite of her nervousness, Hildegard's eyes shone, and Jutta knew the child wasn't imagining things. God had given her a gift, the gift of visions. So Jutta wasn't at all surprised when, as a teenager, Hildegard decided to become a nun and devote her life to God.

In the busy years that followed, Hildegard sang and prayed, spun cloth, studied the Bible, and worked in the garden of the monastery. There the herbs became her special plants. She loved to kneel among them, touch their leaves, and inhale their sharp scents. Sometimes she even nibbled a bit of leaf or flower, just to get to know them with another of her senses. How wonderful they were, these green gifts from God, she thought. And how useful too, for Hildegard soon discovered that she also had the gift of using herbs to heal sick people.

Meanwhile, God continued to send her visions. But Hildegard rarely spoke of them. Other people didn't seem to understand or didn't want to hear about them. Many refused to believe that God would send visions to a woman. So Hildegard kept her visions to herself. But part of her cried out at the wrongness of her silence.

Then, when she was forty-two, she became so ill that she could not leave her bed. By then, Jutta was dead and Hildegard led the small group of nuns.

"I'm so sorry," she gasped to the other sisters. "I can't do a thing for you. I am beaten down by many illnesses. I feel pressed down under the whip of God."

In her illness, Hildegard received yet another vision. A voice from heaven spoke to her.

"O weak person," it said, "speak and write what you see and hear."

Speak and write? The very words terrified Hildegard. She had kept her visions inside for so long. But she struggled from her bed, ready to obey. At once she felt well, full of strength and power.

Since she could not write the most educated type of Latin, the monastery assigned a kindly monk to help her. Hildegard also described pictures to go with her words and someone, probably another monk, painted them.

It took Hildegard ten years to finish her first book about the visions. Other books followed, and so did poems, songs, an opera, and letters—hundreds of letters. Now that she had begun to speak out, no one could keep her quiet.

"Your words make me feel wonder and happiness," a pope once wrote to her.

"Thank you," Hildegard politely wrote back. "Now,

about the people in your own household. You'd better stop the nasty political games they're playing—fast!"

She wasn't afraid of the fierce German emperor, Frederick Barbarossa, either. "I had a dream about a king who wouldn't open his eyes to the misery around him," she told Frederick in a letter. "And a dark haze came and covered the valley. Ravens and other birds came too and tore everything to pieces."

But Hildegard didn't only speak out about evil. She also told about the good things that could happen if people would only follow God's ways.

"God has arranged the world in a wonderful way," she wrote. "The universe is like a web, with all things connected to one another and to God. If people follow God's ways, no one will be poor or sad. People who follow God's ways become like fountains, bringing life to everyone and everything around them."

Hildegard's visions and writings were full of green too.

She spoke of God's "greening power," which not only made plants grow and thrive, but also made people creative and loving. And one of the pictures in her book of visions shows heaven and earth as they will be when evil is gone. The picture is full of green.

Hildegard believed that a prophet should say what was going on in the present and what could happen in the future as a result. Some of what she wrote about the earth certainly makes her that sort of prophet for today. "Greedy people dare to live without God's greening power," she wrote. "The winds are loaded with the stink of evil. The air belches out people's filthy uncleanliness." And she pleaded, "The earth should not be destroyed!"

People often came to Hildegard for advice and help. When she was eighty, a dying young man begged to be buried in the cemetery at Rupertsberg, where she and her nuns now lived. But because of his sinful life, the young man had been thrown out of the church and forbidden burial on church grounds.

Hildegard pitied the young man, who was sorry for his sins and longed to be taken back into the church. A vision told her to grant his request. So Hildegard gladly had him buried on church ground. She and her nuns carefully smoothed away all signs of his grave so no one could move his body.

When the church authorities found out, they were furious. As punishment, they ordered Hildegard and her nuns to stop holding worship services and to stop singing Christian music.

Hildegard responded with a letter. "Those who silence religious music," she wrote, "will go to a place where they will never hear the angels sing."

The punishment lasted six months. Soon after it was lifted, in 1179, Hildegard died. Some observers said that arcs, circles, and a huge cross made of light glowed in the sky the night she died.

Hildegard was never formally canonized by a pope, but she was officially listed as a saint. In 1979, Pope John Paul II called her "a light to her people and her time." That light still shines, and Hildegard's words still speak to us today.

Hedwig of Poland

A country's geography can be a friend or foe in shaping that country's history. In Poland's case, it has too often been a foe. A huge plain of rich farm land stretches across the middle of Poland, and has sometimes looked very tempting to Germany on the west and Russia on the east. Unfortunately, Poland has no strong natural boundaries—such as high mountains—to make people think twice about invasion. So there have been many bloody chapters in the story of Poland's past.

In 966, Prince Mieszko I accepted Christianity on behalf of Poland. He hoped that the strong Catholic church would protect Poland against invaders. But the church brought Poland additional gifts: better government, cultural riches, and, above all, a deep faith in God that has guided—and continues to guide—the Polish people through their darkest hours.

edwig was born in 1174 to Count Berthold and his wife in Bavaria, Germany. For six years, she lived the life of a golden-haired princess in her father's castle. Then the time came to prepare for her future as a wealthy young woman. So Hedwig's parents took her to a convent at nearby Kissingen, where the nuns would teach her how to be a proper wife for the royal husband that her parents would someday choose.

Hedwig learned another lesson at the convent too. She learned to love God. And, deep down, she wished she could forget about money, royal husbands, and all the rest of it.

She wanted only to live at the convent and serve God there forever. That, however, was not what God—or her parents—had in mind for her.

When Hedwig was twelve, her father came to the convent and informed her that she was to marry Henry the Bearded, Duke of Silesia in Poland.

"What will he be like?" Hedwig must have wondered. "Handsome? Kind? Cruel?"

Perhaps Henry did some wondering too. "Will she be pretty? Clever? Crabby?"

The two young people met for the first time on their wedding day, and they fell in love. Soon Hedwig was rumbling away in the royal carriage to her new home in the east.

Henry, she quickly learned, was a good and religious man. But, like many people, he often didn't notice what was right under his nose. Hedwig, on the other hand, was one of the most noticing people Henry had ever met. She noticed hungry people, cold people, and people suffering in prison. Furthermore, she pointed them out to Henry in such a kind way that he couldn't help thinking he should do something for them.

Then, one day, Hedwig learned that Poland had no place where women could learn to read and write.

"Imagine such a thing!" she said to Henry. "Why, we must start a convent with a school as soon as possible. Perhaps at Trebnitz."

To her astonishment, Henry frowned and turned bright red. "No!" he said. "Hedwig, you've gone too far. If there's one thing Poland doesn't need, it's women who can read and write."

"Why, Henry!" said Hedwig. But she pressed him no further. Instead, she prayed about the convent, leaving the whole matter in God's hands.

The next day, the royal couple went hunting in one of Poland's lovely forests. Henry had ridden ahead of Hedwig when suddenly his horse began to sink into the soft ground of a bog. As the horse sank deeper and deeper, Henry started praying.

"If you help me, Lord, I will give Hedwig her convent. I promise!"

The next moment, so the story goes, Henry's horse jumped free of the oozy ground and brought Henry safely back to Hedwig, who hugged him and thanked him for the convent. As the years went by, she would thank him for many more convents—and hospitals too.

Helping others was just one part of Hedwig and Henry's life together. They also raised a family of six children. And, like Polish rulers before and after them, they spent much of their time worrying about wars. Not only were there the ever-ready invaders, but Poland's own princes often battled each other as well. Conrad of Plok, another Polish ruler, was an especially bitter enemy of Henry's. Once Henry managed to defeat him and took over the beautiful city of Krakow as his reward. When he went to church to thank God for giving him the victory, Conrad sneaked into the church, grabbed Henry, tied him up, and took him away.

When Hedwig heard the news, she hurried after the two

men and soon caught up with them. "All right, you two," she said in the same voice she used when two of her sons were fighting over a toy. "This is ridiculous. You are both Poles. You've got plenty of other enemies without fighting one another. Now, I have an idea. Conrad, why don't two of your sons marry two of our daughters? Then we'll all be family. We can put an end to this fighting."

Both Henry and Conrad thought this was an excellent idea. We don't know what the sons and daughters thought, but the marriages were arranged and there was peace at least for a time.

When Henry died in 1238, his death did not devastate Hedwig the way some thought it would. She firmly believed that the two of them would be together again in heaven. Meanwhile, Hedwig decided to make her home in the convent at Trebnitz that Henry had built for her many years ago.

As she settled into the convent, which her own daughter Gertrude now led as abbess, Hedwig's thoughts must have drifted back to her girlhood and the years she spent with the nuns at Kissingen. At that time, she would have given anything to become a nun herself and quietly serve God in the convent.

But it was too late now to live out that old dream. She had spent too much time in the outside world and noticed too much suffering. And she had seen how God could use her to ease that suffering. Henry had left her with a fortune and she would use it to help people. So, although Hedwig made her home in the convent, she did not become a nun.

She lived on for five years after Henry died, long enough to see her son rule as Henry the Good. Then, one day in 1243, she told the nuns to call a priest for her right away.

"I am going to die," she said.

"But there is nothing at all the matter with you!" protested the nuns.

"Please, just send for the priest," Hedwig insisted.

So the priest came and gave her the last rites of the church.

"Look!" cried Hedwig as he finished. "A whole procession of angels is coming in!" And then she died, at the age of sixty-nine.

Hedwig was canonized in 1267 and is still much loved by Polish Christians today. Unlike many of the country's invaders, this golden-haired princess from Bavaria brought Poland nothing but good.

Francis of Assisi

From behind high walls on wooded mountain slopes in the heart of Italy, the ancient town of Assisi kept close watch on nearby Perugia. During the Middle Ages, each Italian town was a city-state, with fiercely loyal citizens ready to grab their weapons at the first hint of disagreement with another city-state. Meanwhile, the Christian countries of Europe felt threatened by Muslims who lived in the Bible lands of Asia to the south and east. Armies of crusaders set out to take over those lands and convert the Muslims—at swordpoint if necessary. Some of Assisi's young men proudly joined those ranks of fighting Crusaders.

But life in Assisi was not all warfare and violence. People also found time to buy and sell and prosper—or to beg if they were poor. And there was time to worship God, to listen to birdsong, and to raise families.

hen Francis was born in 1182, his parents, Pietro and Pica Bernardone, named him John. But Pietro, a cloth merchant with connections in other countries, taught him French while he was still a toddler. So the people of Assisi nicknamed him Francesco (Frenchman) or, in English, Francis.

Young Francis was full of fun and energy, but he wasn't too fond of school. "A typical boy," said his proud papa, who planned to take him into the family business and saw little use for school.

As Francis grew older, ambitions of his own began to stir.

"I'll be a poet," he thought. "No, a soldier. Well, maybe both. Oh, I can decide later. Now, what shall I wear to the party tonight?" Because of the charming way he had of making everyone he met feel important, Francis went to many parties and had many friends.

Then, one day, a quarrel flared up between Assisi and Perugia. Francis and his friends could hardly wait to join the fighting, but their high spirits didn't last long. Perugian troops captured them and kept them in prison for a year. When Francis was finally freed, he had changed. He was still friendly and charming, but his time in prison had made him look at things differently. He began to think deeply about what he saw, and he saw new beauty and new meaning in all of God's creation.

Once, when he was out riding his horse, Francis saw a leper stumbling toward him. Leprosy was a painful disease, and it was believed to be contagious. Lepers were outcasts, whom no sane person would go near. But as Francis watched this man approach, something strange happened. The man's disease and deformity seemed unimportant. Here was a fellow human, a creature of God. Francis leaped from his horse, pressed money into the leper's hand, then raised that hand to his lips and kissed it, a sign of respect.

"I see Christ in you," he whispered and hugged the man.

The leper was deeply moved, and he embraced Francis. "The peace of Christ be with you," he said.

Soon after, Francis was praying in the ramshackle little church of St. Damian when he heard a voice say, "Francis, thou shalt repair my church."

"So!" thought Francis. "God intends for me to rebuild St. Damian's. How glorious!" He promptly sold his horse to get money for materials. He also sold several bolts of his father's fine cloth for extra money. Surely Pietro would want to be part of this glorious mission, Francis thought.

But Pietro was furious. He locked Francis up like a prisoner and finally took him before the local bishop.

"You must give back the money you earned from selling the cloth," the bishop told Francis gently.

Instead of protesting, Francis took off all his fine clothes and piled them before his father. Then he took the money he had gathered and put it on top of the clothes.

"Until this time I have called Pietro Bernardone father," he declared, "but now I am the servant of God."

It was midwinter, and the bishop snatched up a servant's cloak to wrap around the naked young man. But Francis didn't even notice the cold. Off he strode into the woods, homeless and penniless. As he walked, he sang. He was now utterly free to serve God, and his heart nearly burst with joy.

For a while, he repaired other tumble-down churches, begging for building stones as well as for scraps of food to eat. Eventually some friends joined him in his work, and they became known as the Little Brothers. They must own nothing, Francis insisted, because that was the only way they could be totally free. So, in their bare feet and wearing simple grey robes belted with ropes, the Little Brothers set out to tell people about Jesus and to care for the poor. The joy that filled Francis spilled over on all of them and drew more and more followers.

Francis's love for God and for the poor and outcast of society strengthened and deepened with each passing year. But he still had plenty of love to spare for animals and other creatures of nature. "Not only did God make them," he said, "but each of them in its own way lifts my thoughts to their Creator."

During a preaching trip in Italy, he and two other brothers came to a field full of birds. "Wait while I preach to my little sisters, the birds," said Francis as he walked into the field. The birds must have felt his love, because they showed no trace of fear, not even when his robe brushed against them.

"My little sisters," he told them, "you owe much to God, your Creator, and you ought to sing His praise at all times and in all places." When he'd finished his sermon, Francis blessed the birds and they flew away singing.

Another time, Francis came to the town of Gubbio where a wolf had been terrorizing—even eating—the people. Alone outside the town, Francis called, "Come, Brother Wolf. I command you, in the name of Christ, not to hurt me or anyone else."

Instead of leaping on him, the wolf huddled at his feet. As Francis looked at the cowering animal, he was filled with love. Here was a starving, desperate creature of God.

"If I ask the townspeople to feed you regularly, will you stop harming them?"

The wolf sat up, nodded, and placed its paw in Francis's hand as a pledge. Then, meek as a lamb, it followed him into the town. The astonished people promised faithfully to feed the wolf and did so until the creature died, greatly mourned, two years later. Although some say this is merely a legend, many years later, people found the grave of a very large wolf in an old Gubbio church.

One Christmas, Francis wanted to do something special for the humble valley town of Greccio. So he had a stable built up on the mountain. In it he put an altar, a straw-filled manger, and a live ox and donkey. Then he invited the people of Greccio to a midnight service. Up the mountain they came, candles twinkling and children shouting when they caught sight of the stable. At last everyone knelt down on a carpet of pine needles to praise God and thank him for the gift of his Son.

In 1226, the saint who loved all of God's creatures could welcome even Sister Death. Knowing that he was dying, Francis asked to be put on the bare ground in the village of Portiuncula. As he lay there he sang Psalm 142: "Set me free from my prison, so that I may praise Thy name." After he died, the music went on. For, it is said, a huge flock of birds flew overhead and filled the evening sky with their song of thanks and praise.

Francis of Assisi was canonized in 1228 and members of his Franciscan order continue to do great good around the world. Francis had indeed obeyed the command to repair God's church—but not only with stones and mortar. He led many church people to put aside possessions and serve the poor as Jesus himself once did.

Clare of Assisi

Life for a rich girl in Europe during the Middle Ages wasn't easy. True, rich girls lived in lovely homes, wore beautiful clothes and ate fine foods. Some received a smattering of education, many learned to sew, and a few dabbled in music. But mostly they sat idly by, waiting to get married—usually to some rich man chosen by their parents. Those who didn't marry were expected to enter a convent, where, between prayers, they sat around, sewed, and gossiped. Life for a rich girl was boring—especially if the girl had a mind and ambitions of her own.

Clare was a girl with a mind and ambitions of her own. Born in 1193 to Favorino Scefi, a wealthy nobleman, and his wife, the Lady Ortolana, she spent her childhood with her brother and sisters at the Scefi family castle in the mountains or at their beautiful home in Assisi, Italy.

At home, Clare was sheltered from much news of the world. But Assisi was a small town, and she soon heard about that strange young man Francis Bernardone. She was about twelve years old when Francis gave up all his possessions and set out joyfully to serve God by caring for the poor. In Clare's mind, Francis was a hero.

"I want to serve the poor," she told her family when she was fifteen.

They stared at her.

"I want to put aside some of my own food and take it to poor people in Assisi," she explained patiently.

Perhaps for the first time, Clare's parents saw how stubborn she could be, and they gave in. So Clare tied back her golden hair, put on her plainest gown, and went out with baskets of food and words of sympathy for Assisi's poor people. She thought of herself as their servant. And they loved her for her kindness.

As time went by, Clare realized that sharing her food was not enough. God meant her to do more. She decided to serve God completely, as Francis did. With the help of her Aunt Bianca, she met with Francis several times, and the two of them worked out a plan.

One spring night in 1212, eighteen-year-old Clare slipped out of her parents' home. Together, she and Aunt Bianca crept out of Assisi and through the forest to the nearby town of Portiuncula, where Francis and his followers were staying. At the door of the church there, the Little Brothers met them with lighted candles and hymns of praise to God. Standing by the altar, Clare exchanged her rich dress for a poor grey robe, and Francis himself cut off her long hair as a sign of her devotion to God. She was Sister Clare now.

That night, Francis took her to a nearby convent to stay until he could find her a place of her own. The next day, however, Clare's family caught up with her and demanded that she return home. Clare fled to the convent church and held tight to the altar.

"You're coming home with us," roared her father. "You don't belong here. We have a fine man ready to marry you."

"No!" cried Clare. "I belong to God now. You can't take me away." And she threw back her hood and showed them her cropped hair.

Her father took one look and turned away, defeated. But his fury returned a few days later when Clare's fifteen-year-old sister, Agnes, ran away to join her. Eleven other men from the Scefi family accompanied Favorino when he went to bring Agnes home. They were dragging her away when tiny Agnes fell to the ground and screamed for help. Clare rushed to her rescue.

With her eyes blazing and her jaw firmly set, Clare faced her family. "Go home!" she commanded the men. Meekly, they went.

A year later, Clare and Agnes had their own convent, the house and church of St. Damian's that Francis had rebuilt with his own hands. Soon the order of "Poor Clares" began to grow, first at St.Damian's, then in other places. Aunt Bianca was one of the first women to join. Later, after Clare's father died, her mother and younger sister, Beatrice, also joined the Poor Clares.

But Clare faced one great disappointment in her new life. She had hoped to go out into the world—to nurse lepers and to convert unbelievers as Francis did. Instead, Francis told her that she and her nuns could serve God best by never leaving the convent grounds. Sick people would be brought to them for care. They could sew furnishings for the churches of the poor. Most important, they could spend long, long hours in prayer and worship.

So that is what the Poor Clares did. And poor they were—owning nothing for themselves. They slept on simple mats with wooden pillows. They ate food from their garden or shared scraps that Francis and the Little Brothers begged from townspeople. Now and then, a pope would hear of their work and try to make their lives easier. But Clare always said no—and won.

In spite of her longing to serve God in the darkest corners of the earth, Clare's greatest gift turned out to be prayer. Beggars and popes, royalty and peasants all asked for her prayers. And she prayed for them all. Like Francis, Clare saw every person as a creature of God.

Through all her years in the convent, Clare almost never saw Francis himself; such a thing would not look right in the eyes of the world. Once, though, toward the end of his life when he was in pain and almost blind, Francis rested awhile at St. Damian's. It was during this time that he wrote his famous canticle: "Praised be my Lord God with all his creatures... "

The words of Francis's song touched Clare deeply. She, too, saw God's hand in all the things of nature. Some of her happiest moments were spent in the tiny convent garden where she planted roses, lilies, and violets.

Clare lived for twenty-seven years after Francis died, although she was ill during most of this time. Once she lay sick on her mat while war raged in Italy. Suddenly her nuns came running to her.

"Mother!" cried one. "Enemy archers have surrounded the convent! What shall we do?"

"Carry me to the doorway," said Clare calmly. There she knelt and prayed, "Protect them, good Lord, I beseech you, whom I at this hour am not able to protect."

And God's voice answered her, "I will always be your guardian."

Miraculously, the archers turned and left. Clare's prayer had been answered.

In 1253, when she was sixty, Clare's tired body failed. Her sister Agnes, who now led a group of Poor Clares in another area, came to be with her. So did three of the Little Brothers. Toward the end, they and her nuns were gathered around the couch where Clare lay. Suddenly they heard her speak in a soft voice: "Go forth, Christian soul, go forth without fear, for you have a good guide for your journey. Go forth without fear, for he that created you has sanctified you, always has he protected you, and he loves you with the love of a mother."

"To whom are you speaking, Mother?" asked a nun.

"I am talking to my own soul," said Clare. Then she turned to another nun. "Can you see the King of Glory whom I see?" she asked. A moment later, she died.

Clare of Assisi was canonized in 1255. She had escaped the boredom of riches for a hard life of faithful service. And because of her faithfulness, God made her a blessing to countless people.

Elizabeth of Hungary

Power and the getting of power have always played a major role in the history of the world, often at the expense of human lives and human happiness. Central Europe in the thirteenth century was no exception. In a bewildering hodge-podge of kingdoms, princedoms, and other political groups, rulers used whatever means they could to consolidate and expand their own influence. One of their favorite means was marrying their children to one another. Infants were pledged to marry other infants, and toddlers to marry teenagers, so that both families might profit from the marriage. Such was the fate of little Elizabeth before she was even one day old.

The great Klingsor, a minstrel, first told the story one night in 1207. He had come to the town of Eisenach, in Thuringia (a part of Germany), to judge a singing contest of other minstrels, and he brought exciting news.

"A daughter has been born to Queen Gertrude and King Andrew II of Hungary," Klingsor announced. "She will be called Elizabeth, and she will marry Prince Ludwig of Thuringia. And one day she will become a saint."

Prince Herman of Thuringia, Ludwig's father, took this announcement very seriously. Alliance with Hungary would be a fine thing for Thuringia, and it would strengthen his own family's position. Elizabeth's father felt the same; Klingsor had told him a lot about the riches of Thuringia.

So when Princess Elizabeth was four, a company of knights and female servants trundled her off across the mountains to Thuringia, to be raised in Wartburg Castle with her eleven-year-old fiancé. She never again saw her mother, who was murdered a few years later. Her father forgot that she existed.

Still, Elizabeth lived a happy life, at least for a while. She had plenty of other children to play with, and she and Ludwig genuinely liked one another. She also loved to pray and to serve God by doing kind things for the poor people who lived in Eisenach, at the foot of the mountain on which Wartburg Castle stood. Prince Herman gave her a generous allowance, which she promptly spent on food and clothes for those who needed them. Sometimes she even carried food from the castle kitchens down the mountain to hungry children in Eisenach.

Herman heartily approved of all this, but unfortunately he died when Elizabeth was only nine. His wife, Princess Sophia, found her future daughter-in-law's actions highly irritating.

"Why can't you behave more like a princess?" she asked. "Can't you see that everyone is laughing at you?"

Soon others at court *were* laughing at Elizabeth—just to please the powerful Sophia. As the years went by, Elizabeth began to wonder if Ludwig might be laughing at her too. He spent a great deal of his time away on royal business, and some people said he would never marry that strange girl from Hungary. But they didn't know Ludwig's heart.

"I would not desert Elizabeth for an entire mountain of gold," he told one of his knights. And, in 1220, when Elizabeth was thirteen and Ludwig was twenty, the two of them were married.

That was the start of seven wonderful years for Elizabeth. Like his father, Ludwig approved of her kindness to poor people, even when she feared he might not. Once, says the most famous legend about Elizabeth, she and her maid were coming down the path from the castle, carrying loaves of bread wrapped in their cloaks. Suddenly they met Ludwig.

"What are you hiding there?" Ludwig teased his wife.

All those years of Sophia's cruelty flashed through Elizabeth's mind. Maybe Ludwig would think she wasn't acting like a princess either. So she pulled her cloak more closely around her, hoping to hide the bread.

But Ludwig, still teasing, twitched open the cloak. To everyone's astonishment, instead of bread, a heap of roses and lilies tumbled onto the path.

At another time during her marriage, Elizabeth was horrified by the sight of a man dying of leprosy in a tumble-down shed. She helped him to the castle and settled him in Ludwig's bed, where she could nurse him. Sophia was beside herself with rage.

"Look at what that wife of yours has done now!" she shrieked at Ludwig, dragging him to the room and pointing to the bed.

Ludwig looked at the dying man whom Elizabeth had

been nursing. Then, very quietly, he said, "I see Christ."

Elizabeth served poor people in many other ways as well. At least nine hundred people climbed the mountain each day to beg for food at the castle gates. Elizabeth made sure they received it. She also founded two hospitals, and took care of many orphans.

Elizabeth and Ludwig had two children, a boy and a girl, and were expecting their third when Ludwig decided to join Emperor Frederick II on a crusade to the Holy Land. He went no farther than Italy, though, where he came down with bubonic plague. Just after the birth of her second daughter, Elizabeth learned that Ludwig was dead.

What happened next has become somewhat confused over the years. It seems that Ludwig's brother, Henry, was so eager to take power that he forced Elizabeth and her three children to leave the castle in the dead of winter. They wandered aimlessly, first staying at a shabby inn, then with a poor priest who could offer them only beds of clean straw.

Even Sophia was shocked by what her younger son had done, and she tried to help Elizabeth as best she could. Eventually, some of Ludwig's knights forced Henry to stop persecuting Elizabeth. She then was allowed to live in a small wooden house with her children and the two maids who had been with her ever since she left Hungary.

Even then Elizabeth's troubles were not over. Some time earlier, she had sought spiritual help from a priest called Conrad of Marburg, who was to be her guide in all religious matters. Having so much power over another person at last went to Conrad's head, though, and he became cruel to

Elizabeth. He slapped and beat her and later sent away her children and her maids. Elizabeth never saw them again. Now, the girl who had once been a princess had to spin cloth to earn money for the little food she ate and for what she needed to care for poor and sick people.

So many hardships caused Elizabeth's health to fail, and, in 1231, she went to bed with a high fever. One evening, legend says, a woman sitting beside her heard music coming from Elizabeth's bed.

"It was a little bird," Elizabeth told her later. "His song has filled me with great happiness. He told me that I will die in three days."

Three days later, Elizabeth of Hungary died, at the age of twenty-three. She was canonized four years later. Her brief life was nothing like that of a fairy-tale princess. But it was a glowing example of someone whose great love for God led her to love and serve others, receiving the love of countless people in return.

Bridget of Sweden

During the Middle Ages, getting from one place to another was no fun. Sea travel was terribly dangerous. On land, the rich might ride in beautiful carriages, but they still considered themselves lucky if their teeth weren't jounced out of their heads on the primitive roads. The less rich had to be satisfied with travel in wooden wagons or on horse or mule. Poor folk, of course, walked. But in spite of the distances and difficulties separating people, the countries of Western Europe were united by the Roman Catholic faith—the official religion of the time. So the need for more convents and monasteries and the quarrel over whether or not the pope should live in Rome were issues that concerned people in Sweden just as much as they concerned the people living in Italy.

B ridget was born in Sweden around 1303. Her father was governor of Sweden's principal province, Upland, and that made him an important man. Bridget, her family assumed, would grow up to be a fine lady. When she was thirteen, she fulfilled their ambitions by marrying Ulf Godmarsson, the eighteen-year-old son of another important man. The young couple lived together happily in a large castle on Ulf's estate and eventually had eight children, four girls and four boys.

But, even early in her marriage, something about Bridget set her apart from most other fine ladies of her day. She was interested in learning—very interested—and made friends with as many well-educated people as she could.

When she was thirty-two, Bridget found herself saddled with a chore reserved for fine ladies. She was asked to go to the court of the king of Sweden, Magnus II, and become lady-in-waiting to his young wife, Blanche. This sudden immersion in court life, with all its frivolities and intrigues, did not please the serious Bridget. She could see that Magnus was not a good man, and Blanche couldn't hold a serious thought in her head for more than a minute.

By this time, Bridget was already having visions, which she believed came from God. She called her visions "revelations" and was not timid about sharing what she learned in them with whomever she thought needed the information. Some of the revelations concerned practical matters: "People would be much healthier if they washed themselves." Others involved politics: "The peace treaty between England and France should work thus-and-so." Still others led Bridget to tell the king and queen how they might improve their spiritual lives.

No one at court paid much attention to what she said. Instead, they turned her into a joke.

"What was the Lady Bridget dreaming about last night?" one lady would ask another, and both would snicker.

Bridget had other troubles too. Her oldest daughter married a terrible man. Her youngest son died. During a leave of absence from the court, Bridget and her husband went on a pilgrimage to visit religious sites in Spain. On their way home, Ulf became very ill, and he died at a monastery at Alvastra, Sweden.

Bridget stayed at Alvastra for a while, and there she received more visions. One told her to build a convent near the town of Vadstena. Another said she must warn King Magnus one more time to mend his ways.

Bridget began with Magnus. While she was at it, she extended her warning to include Blanche, the nobles, and some bishops of the church as well. Amazingly enough, Magnus listened to her. He changed his way of life (at least for the time being) and gave Bridget a great deal of money with which to build her convent.

So Bridget got started on the convent right away. She arranged for it to house sixty nuns, but built separate quarters for twenty-five men as well. Her group became known as the Order of the Most Holy Saviour, or the Bridgettines. The rules that the nuns and monks lived by were much like those followed at other convents, except that each person could have all the books that she or he wanted to study. Learning was still important to Bridget.

Then, at the age of forty-six, she left her convent and set out for Rome, in obedience to another of her visions. That must have taken some courage, since the deadly bubonic plague was again running rampant through Europe. Even though she would have been much safer at home, Bridget was never short on courage.

The popes had moved their headquarters from Rome to Avignon, France, in the early 1300s. Bridget, as well as many others, firmly believed that the head of the church belonged in Rome. And, as usual, Bridget didn't hesitate to say what she thought. People in Rome were used to hearing strong talk about the popes, so they didn't pay too much attention to Bridget at first. But when she started speaking out about the immoral actions she saw in the people around her, she became less and less popular. She probably didn't even notice. Popularity was always one of the last things on Bridget's mind.

During much of her time in Rome, Bridget had little or no money, and sometimes she even had to beg for food. But, instead of worrying about herself, she used what little money she could gather to set up charities for other people.

In 1371, some years after she had returned to Sweden, Bridget received another vision. This one directed her to go on a pilgrimage to the Holy Land, where Jesus had lived and taught. Her daughter Catherine, two of her sons, Charles and Birger, and some friends went with her. They'd gone no further than Naples, Italy, when the first disaster struck them.

"Mother," announced Charles, "the queen of Spain, Joanna, wants to marry me."

"*Marry* you? But, Charles, you already have a wife back in Sweden."

"Well, yes, but... "

"And Queen Joanna already has a husband—her third, if I'm not mistaken—in Spain."

"Well, yes, but... "

Bridget's worries about her son's impending marriage soon shifted to another problem. Charles was taken ill with a high fever. Two weeks later, he died in his mother's arms.

In spite of her grief, Bridget went on with the trip. After surviving a shipwreck at Jaffa, she finally reached the Holy Land. There, legend says, God comforted her in a very special way. As she travelled from place to place, Bridget was given visions in which she was able to see Jesus in the actual sites where he once lived and taught. During these visions, it was as if Bridget had journeyed back in a time machine to Bible days.

But even her visions and her strong faith did not change the fact that Bridget was now seventy years old, worn out from work and grief, and sick besides. She and her group managed to get back to Rome, but that was as far as she would go. On July 23, 1373, Bridget died in Rome at the age of seventy-one. Her body was taken, with great respect, to Sweden for burial.

Bridget was canonized in 1391 and is the patron saint of Sweden. Her daughter Catherine carried on with Bridget's work and, although she was never formally canonized, Catherine too became known as a saint.

Sergius of Radonezh

Russia in the 1300s was not so much a country as a collection of isolated pockets of people, loosely bound together by their common misery and staunch loyalty to the Orthodox church. Sweden, Germany, Poland, and Lithuania had cut them off from Central and Western Europe. Mongols had invaded from the east, imposing harsh taxes and committing whatever atrocities occurred to them. Bubonic plague periodically stalked the land, sometimes wiping out entire cities. Famine reaped its grim harvest as well. Even Russia's own princes couldn't get along with one another and squabbled ceaselessly over property and power.

I n 1314, Sergius was born into a troubled Russia. For a time, he, his parents, Cyril and Mary, and his brothers, Stephen and Peter, lived comfortably in the town of Rostov. Then feuding princes drove them to the village of Radonezh, where they tried to scrape together a living by farming. In spite of these hardships, Cyril and Mary insisted that their boys go to school.

Stephen and Peter did very well there. But no matter how hard he tried, Sergius could not learn to read and write. His parents scolded him, his teacher punished him, his classmates made fun of him, and Sergius himself prayed desperately to God for help. Still, he couldn't learn.

One day, according to legend, Sergius was out looking for a lost foal when he met an old holy man.

"What do you want, child?" asked the man. Sergius thought he looked a lot like paintings of angels he had seen.

"Sir," said Sergius, "more than anything, I want to learn to read and write."

"Hmmm," said the holy man. He prayed for Sergius, then gave him a little piece of sweet-tasting bread. Then they went back to Sergius's home, where the old man prepared to hold a worship service.

"You," he told Sergius, "will read the psalms."

"Me?" squeaked Sergius. But, when the moment came, he read the psalms perfectly. From then on, he could read anything. The family accompanied the holy man to the door, where he suddenly vanished into thin air.

"Maybe he *was* an angel," thought Sergius.

Sergius grew to be a big, strong man, known for his goodness and love of God. He wanted to be a monk, but first he took care of his parents until they died. Then he and his brother Stephen went off into the forests around Moscow. Eventually they found a clearing near a stream, where they built a wooden hut and a small chapel that they dedicated to the Holy Trinity. It was a wild, lonely place, with no people or roads anywhere near, and the brothers had to search for food in the forest. Before long, Stephen decided he'd rather enter a proper monastery in Moscow.

But Sergius loved his wilderness. He made friends with

the forest creatures and soon had a special friendship with a large bear. Now and then, Sergius made bread for his daily meals. One day, he put a slice of bread on a tree stump.

"There, brother," he said to the bear. "You could probably use some dinner, too."

From then on, he and the bear often shared a meal. But one day, Sergius had only one small piece of bread left. He watched the bear come to the stump, sniff, then sit down and look around.

"No food?" the bear seemed to say.

In the end Sergius couldn't stand to watch the bear's disappointment. He gave the bear his last piece of bread and went hungry himself.

After a while, Sergius officially became a monk, and other monks came to live with him. They worked hard to build a monastery in the middle of the forest, with big Sergius working hardest of all. And when they at last were through, the monks demanded that Sergius be their leader, the abbot of the monastery. Sergius protested. But when the monks insisted, he sighed and took the job. Still wearing the most tattered robe of all, he looked more like a peasant than an abbot.

Under Sergius's leadership, Holy Trinity monastery thrived, but church officials soon told Sergius he must run it as other monasteries were run. No monk should own personal possessions and each must be assigned specific duties. Sergius agreed, and for a while all went well. Then the monks began to bicker among themselves. When Sergius heard two of them arguing during a church service, he walked straight out of the chapel and into the forest. He kept walking, too, until he found another wild place, and there he settled down. Other men eventually came to join him, and soon they'd built a new church and a new monastery.

Meanwhile, the monks at Holy Trinity were feeling ashamed of themselves.

"We're like sheep without a shepherd," they told a church official. "Please send Sergius back to us."

"You had better go back," the official said to Sergius. "I'll find someone else to run the new monastery."

So Sergius tramped back to Holy Trinity where he was met by some very sheepish—but very happy—monks.

By 1378, Sergius had founded other monasteries and word of his goodness and wisdom had spread throughout Russia. One day, Metropolitan Alexis, one of the highest officials in the church, asked Sergius to visit him in Moscow.

"Sergius," he said, "I am near death, and everyone wants you to be metropolitan after me."

"Oh, no!" replied Sergius. "Such a thing is beyond my powers."

Alexis pleaded, but Sergius would not give in.

"God wants me to serve him as I am," he said and went back to his forest.

In 1380, Dmitry Donskoy, Prince of Moscow, came galloping out to Holy Trinity to talk to Sergius.

"Word has reached me," panted the prince, "that Khan Mamai and his Mongol hordes are about to attack us again. Do I dare take my men and fight against them?"

"Do it," said Sergius, "and don't be afraid. God will be on your side."

His words filled the prince and his soldiers with courage. Although many died in the fighting, they defeated the Mongols at Kulikovo, the first victory the Russians ever won over these invaders. In thanksgiving for the prayers of Sergius and his monks, Prince Dmitry built yet another monastery.

Sergius's fame even reached the ears of a Greek bishop, who refused to believe that such a holy person could come from such a savage place as Russia. He had to see for himself. According to one story, the moment the bishop caught sight of Sergius, he became blind. It was only after Sergius touched his eyes that he could see again.

"I have beheld a holy man and an angel on earth," declared the bishop.

Sergius remained strong and active until the last six months of his life. When he did die, in 1392, it was in his own monastery and with a prayer on his lips. Some even say that angels surrounded him and opened the gates of heaven so he could go in.

Sergius of Radonezh was canonized sometime before 1449 and became the patron saint of Moscow. He remains a beloved saint in Russia even today.

Catherine of Siena

Near the beginning of the 1300s, the pope, head of the Catholic church, chose to make his home at Avignon, in France, instead of Rome, where popes had always lived before. Other popes followed his example. The French were delighted, since more and more Frenchmen became high church officials. But almost everyone else in Europe thought the pope should return to Rome at once. Some of Italy's city-states became so angry with the pope's departure that they actually fought armed battles with the representatives of the pope. Obviously, someone needed to make peace, so the church could get back to its real business again. But peacemaking in this situation would be difficult, perhaps too tricky for any one human being.

Catherine Benincasa was born in 1347, the twenty-fourth (and next to last) child of Giacomo and Lapa, wealthy wool dyers in the town of Siena. Although Catherine was a friendly, cheerful child, she also liked to spend time alone—which couldn't have been easy with more than twenty brothers and sisters.

Once, when she was about seven, she and her older brother Stephen were watching the sun set over the Church of St. Dominic, just up the hill from their home. Suddenly, Catherine saw more than brilliant streaks of red, rose, and gold from the setting sun. She saw Jesus, sitting on a throne in the sky, with his friends Peter, Paul, and John around him. Jesus reached out his hand and blessed her and then...

"Are you all right?" Stephen was shaking her as hard as he could. "Are you all right, Catherine?"

Catherine jumped, took one more look at the sky, and began to cry.

"Why did you do that?" she sobbed. "Now he's not there anymore."

"Who?" asked Stephen. He hadn't seen anyone. "Catherine you weren't even breathing!"

But Catherine wouldn't tell him whom she'd seen. That would be her secret. She felt, though, that from then on she belonged to Jesus. She knew she would spend the rest of her life serving him.

In those days, Italian girls usually married in their early teens. So when Catherine, aged twelve, informed her mother that she was not going to marry anyone—but serve Jesus instead—Lapa thought her child was talking nonsense.

"I must show her that I'm serious," thought Catherine. And she promptly chopped off her long hair to make herself as undesirable as possible.

Lapa and Giacomo were beside themselves.

"All right!" they shouted. "If you're not going to become a wife, you can just get busy doing servant's work around here. And you can give up your private bedroom and sleep with the rest of your sisters."

Her parents thought Catherine would hate doing the chores and losing her privacy, but to their surprise, she didn't seem at all upset. She even did the dirtiest jobs around the house as happily as if she were picking flowers in a meadow.

Giacomo couldn't stay angry in the face of Catherine's happy attitude, and he finally gave in.

"Serve Jesus if you want to," he told her, giving her back her private bedroom.

When she was eighteen, Catherine joined the Third Order of the Dominicans. That meant she was a nun and wore a nun's robes, but she lived at home instead of in a convent. For the next three years, she spent her time in her bedroom, eating and sleeping little, and speaking only to God in prayer. During that period, she mysteriously learned to read; some say God simply gave her the gift of reading.

Then, Catherine had another vision of Jesus. This time she saw him handing her a gold ring—the symbol of marriage—and she knew she had made the right choice as a child. She also decided it was time to go out into the world and help care for poor and sick people, just as Jesus did.

As she went about her new work, Catherine was once again the happy, outgoing person she had been as a child. She nursed suffering lepers and cheered up cranky old people. She visited prisoners in their filthy cells, settled arguments between enemies, and buried dead people— including, later, her own father. In addition, Catherine continued to have visions of Jesus and periods of great inner emotion, called raptures. Gradually, friends and followers were drawn to her. They became a second family that stayed with her for the rest of her life.

It was Catherine's spreading fame as a peacemaker that

eventually got her involved in religious politics. Because
so many people visited or wrote to ask for her advice, she
began dictating letters of her own to send. (Although she
could read, Catherine had never learned how to write.)
Among the letters she sent were words of advice to Pope
Gregory XI in Avignon. Once she even sent the pope
candied orange peel as a Christmas gift. "The taste is first
bitter, then sweet," she said in a note accompanying the
gift. "That is how it is when you do God's will, too. And
God's will is that you return to Rome."

Although not all of Catherine's adventures in politics
turned out well, she did enjoy a resounding success with
Pope Gregory. He'd been thinking about returning to
Rome anyway, and Catherine's good-humored advice
helped him to make up his mind. Unfortunately, he didn't
live very long after he got there, and his death brought
fresh troubles to the church.

One new pope was chosen in Rome, while a different
one was chosen in Avignon. Everyone began fighting with
everyone else about who was the real pope. It was a battle
of opinions that lasted forty years. Catherine, of course, felt
that the man elected in Rome, Urban VI, was God's choice.
And she sent a whole blizzard of letters supporting him.

She also sent letters to Urban himself, suggesting that he
might win more friends if he were just a little more gentle
in his ways. Urban didn't seem to mind this criticism in the
least. In fact, he invited Catherine to come to Rome, and he
told his officials to pay attention to what she said.

In addition to her many letters, Catherine dictated an

important book called *The Dialogue*. In it, a person asks God questions and God tells her many things. Catherine believed that God dictated the book to her, just as she dictated it to her helpers. In the book, she explains that when she is close to God, she learns the truth about him and his love for her. That truth fills her with love, which she shares with God's people. Sharing love makes her feel close to God again, where she learns more of the truth about him—and on and on and on. It was like a circle with no beginning and no end.

Catherine lived what she said in *The Dialogue*. Her life was a circle of prayer and caring for God's people, over and over again. She never did succeed in bringing peace to the church. But her life and words have inspired many people and nourished the hope for peace in many hearts.

By 1380, Catherine's body was worn out. Although she was only thirty-three, she had suffered a series of strokes. Finally, on April 29, while in Rome, she died. There is a story that when she looked out at the sky on the evening of her death, she saw Jesus on his throne, along with Peter, Paul, and John. But this time no one shook her from her reverie, and so the vision did not go away.

Catherine of Siena was canonized in 1461 and, in 1970, along with Teresa of Avila, was one of the first two women to be named a Doctor of the Church.

Joan of Arc

In 1337, King Edward III of England boldly proclaimed that he was also the rightful king of France. When he attempted to claim parts of France as his own, the Hundred Years' War began. This was actually a series of wars, complicated by civil war in France, peasant rebellions in both France and England, and huge outbreaks of bubonic plague. By 1380, France was in bad shape and King Charles VI, who was insane, did little to help. After his death, his eldest son could not even be crowned Charles VII. To be official, the coronation had to take place in the city of Rheims, and enemy forces blocked all routes into Rheims.

he little village of Domrémy in the Champagne area of France had felt its share of the burdens of war. Certainly none of the villagers could possibly have guessed that the baby born to Jacques d'Arc and his wife in 1412 would someday be God's instrument for ending the struggles.

The baby was a girl named Jeanne ("Joan" in English), and she spent her childhood days doing the same things the other village children did. Although she didn't learn to read and write, Joan's mother taught her to spin thread and sew. Sometimes Joan watched over her father's sheep, and sometimes she sang and danced with her friends.

Suddenly, when Joan was thirteen, she saw a blaze of light and heard a voice from heaven. She was standing in her family's garden and the voice said, "Be a good girl and go to church." The experience almost scared young Joan out of her wits.

As time went by, Joan heard more voices and eventually had visions in which she saw St. Michael, St. Catherine, and St. Margaret. "You must help France," they told her, "and you must begin by talking to Robert Baudricourt, commander of the king's forces."

"But I'm a poor peasant girl!" protested Joan. "I can't fight. I can't even ride a horse."

"God commands it," replied the voices.

So Joan persuaded an uncle of hers to introduce her to Baudricourt, who was stationed in a nearby town. But when she'd explained why she'd come to see him, Baudricourt laughed at her and sent her home.

Still, the voices persisted, and so did Joan. The second time she visited Baudricourt, he began to think there might be truth in what she said. Under his protection, she went to Chinon, where Charles, the heir to the throne, was staying.

Charles had been forewarned of Joan's mission, and he decided to play a trick on the young peasant girl. Before she arrived, he traded his royal clothes for the clothes of his servant. Then he waited for Joan to appear and make a fool of herself by speaking to the wrong person.

As soon as Joan arrived, she stepped down from her horse and marched right up to Charles.

"Oh, I'm not in charge," Charles said with a smile. "The heir to the throne is over there."

"No, fair sire," replied Joan. "I know that you are the man I seek. I have come on important business—not foolishness—and I will not leave until you hear my request." Then she informed Charles that she wanted to lead a group of soldiers to rescue the city of Orleans, which was under siege by enemy forces.

Charles was deeply impressed by Joan, and he was tempted to give her the soldiers. But many people in his court tried to convince him that she was insane. So he sent her to be questioned by a group of church officials in Poitiers. These men talked with Joan, as well as with people who knew her. Three weeks later, they declared that nothing was wrong with her.

So Joan got her soldiers as well as a great black horse, a suit of white metal, and a banner with the names *Jesus* and *Mary* on it. She got a sword, too, but she did not want to use it.

"Forward! Forward!" she cried in her clear, young voice. And, without question, some 12,000 soldiers followed her into battle. In less than two weeks, Orleans was free. Although Joan received a serious shoulder wound, she pressed on to other victories, always led by the voices God sent her.

At last the road to Rheims was cleared of enemy forces, and on July 17, 1429, Joan stood beside Charles VII at his coronation. "Gentle king," she said, "now the will of God is accomplished."

Joan had done all that her voices demanded of her. From then on they spoke no more. Joan won no more battles either. The new king failed to support her efforts to free Paris and her plan failed.

In May of 1430, Joan led her men to help the town of Compiègne, which was under attack from the Burgundians, fellow Frenchmen who sided with the English invaders. She entered the city on May 23, but, later that day, she was forced to retreat. As she tried to escape, Joan found that the drawbridge leading out of the city had been raised. She was trapped. A Burgundian soldier pulled her from her horse and made her a prisoner of the Duke of Burgundy.

Charles VII could have bargained for her release. But, in spite of all she had done for him, neither he nor any of his people made any attempt to help her. They pretended that she did not exist.

The English knew she existed, though, and they were eager to get rid of this formidable enemy once and for all. They bought her from the Duke of Burgundy and put her on trial as a sorceress and a heretic.

The trial dragged on for months. Meanwhile Joan's captors kept her in chains, guarded by five cruel soldiers who made fun of her.

"Admit that your so-called voices are from the devil and you will live," demanded her judges. "Keep saying that they come from God and you will be burned at the stake."

Just once Joan wavered—she was so alone and so frightened—but she quickly stood firm again. Her voices were from God and she would not deny them.

On May 30, 1431, as 10,000 men watched, nineteen-year-old Joan of Arc was taken to the marketplace at Rouen, tied to a stake, and burned to death. It did not take very long. A brave priest held up a cross before her and Joan looked steadfastly at it. Then, in a loud voice, she cried, "Jesus!" and died. Some of the bystanders cried. Others tried to laugh.

"We are undone," said a secretary to the English king. "We have burned a saint."

In 1453, the Hundred Years' War ended, mostly thanks to Joan's triumphs on the battlefield. In 1456, Pope Callistus III appointed a commission that declared her innocent of all the charges that had been brought against her. On May 16, 1920, Joan of Arc was canonized.

Angela Merici

By the late 1400s, Italy's assorted city-states were still feuding with one another, as they had been for hundreds of years. In addition, the people within each city-state were also fighting among themselves. Almost every city had two political parties who couldn't agree about anything. Other European rulers quickly saw that so much internal bickering made Italy easy prey for invasion, and soon both French and Spanish forces were pouncing on one city after another. All this turmoil brought great hardships to many Italian people. And, as is so often the case, the children were the ones who suffered most of all. An embattled land must devote its energies to survival. There is little time for children and the things they need, such as education.

A ngela Merici was born sometime around 1470 in the small town of Desenzano on Lake Garda in northern Italy. There she spent the first ten years of her life.

When she was ten the death of her parents turned Angela's life upside-down. She and her sister and brother went to live with their well-to-do uncle in the town of Salo. Three things helped Angela get through that difficult period: her faith in God, her uncle's kindness, and the fact that she and her sister and brother still had each other.

Then, when Angela was thirteen, death struck again.

This time a sudden illness carried off her older sister so quickly that no one even had a chance to send for a priest. If the priest had been there, Angela knew, he would have listened to her sister confess her sins. Then he would have assured her of forgiveness.

"But there was no priest." That dreadful fact echoed in Angela's mind day and night like a tolling bell. "My sister could not confess her sins and be forgiven. And so she can never go to heaven."

This combination of grief and fear for her sister might have done Angela great harm. But God saw her distress and sent her a vision which showed her that her sister was safe and happy with him. From then on, Angela knew that she would spend her life serving God. "I want to be just like St. Francis of Assisi," she said. "I want to live in poverty and care for poor people."

So, when she was fifteen, she became a tertiary of the Franciscan order. Tertiaries were members of the order who lived in their own homes, not in a convent, but they lived simply and devoted much of their time to prayer and serving the poor. As a sign that she needed only God, Angela gave up almost all of her possessions—even her bed—and limited her meals to bread, vegetables, and water.

Then, when she was nearly twenty-two, her uncle died and Angela decided to go back to Desenzano, the town where she was born. As she visited her old friends, renewing acquaintances and catching up on events, she began to notice something that bothered her deeply.

"The poor children in Desenzano are absolutely

ignorant!" she told some of her friends. "Everyone has forgotten them. Their parents either can't teach them or won't teach them. Why, the children don't even know anything about God!"

"Perhaps the adults have too many other things on their minds," suggested one of her friends.

But Angela could not accept this excuse. "Even so, someone needs to be teaching those children." An idea began to grow in her mind. "Why not us? We could gather together a few of the little girls and give them regular lessons. Think how that would change their lives!"

Young Angela was a small, pretty woman. Like her hero, St. Francis, she could be very charming and very persuasive when she wanted to be. And when she was on fire with an idea, it was almost impossible to say no to her. Soon her school for girls was thriving in Desenzano. It did so well, in fact, that people in the nearby city of Brescia heard of it and asked Angela to come and start a similar school for them.

From then on, Brescia became Angela's home. She made friends with a group of men and women who shared her beliefs and supported her work, and she spent most of her time teaching girls. Now and then, though, Angela would leave her work to visit some religious shrine. She was especially excited when she had a chance to visit the Holy Land with a young relative. It was that trip that led to the story of one of the miracles in her life.

Her group had reached the Greek island of Crete when all at once Angela lost her vision.

"You had better return home," others in the group told

her. "You won't want to go into strange places when you are blind."

"I am going on," said Angela in a voice that permitted no argument, and go on she did. She visited every place the rest of the group visited. Then, on the way home, she paused at Crete to pray in the same place where she had lost her sight. As suddenly as it had gone, her vision returned, and she could see as well as she had before.

In 1525, Angela took a trip to Rome. By then, both she and her work were so well known that she was allowed a visit with the pope, Clement VII.

"Why don't you stay in Rome?" he suggested. "We have a group of nuns who are nurses and who could use someone with your gifts to lead them."

Angela thought about this. It wouldn't be easy to say no to the pope. But she knew that God had not called her to lead nurses; he had called her to teach girls. So she kindly refused and went back to her duties in Brescia.

Unfortunately, she hadn't been back long before war forced her to leave again. All civilians were asked to leave Brescia so that the soldiers could fight freely throughout the city. Angela and some of her friends went to the city of Cremona. In no time she gathered a new group of girls and began teaching again.

Still, she was glad when peace returned and she could go back to Brescia. There, in 1533, she rented a house and began training some of the young women who had been helping her teach.

Two years later, when Angela felt their training had been

completed, she and twenty-eight young women pledged themselves to the service of God. Angela chose St. Ursula as their patron, a saint who was important both to learning and to women. November 25, 1535, became the founding day of the Ursuline order of teachers, an order that still does excellent work today.

At first, it was not a very formal order. Most of Angela's teachers wore black dresses instead of the habits worn by other groups of nuns. Although they met together for classes and to worship God, many of the women still lived with their families. The idea of a group of women serving God by teaching children was new and strange to a lot of people, and Angela knew that the Ursulines must move slowly to give people time to accept them.

The others chose her as head of the group, and she led the Ursulines for five years, until she died in 1540. But it wasn't until four years after her death that Pope Paul III officially recognized Angela's group as the Company of St. Ursula.

No doubt that official recognition would have pleased Angela Merici. But, even unrecognized, she and the many women who worked with her had already accomplished great things. Beginning with those forgotten little girls in Desenzano, the Ursulines could trace a long line of educated women who, thanks to them, now knew and loved God.

John of God

Portugal is a small country compared to Spain, with which it shares the Iberian Peninsula in Western Europe. But in the late 1400s and early 1500s, small Portugal was mighty. King Manuel "the Fortunate" reigned, Vasco da Gama found a Cape route to India and its riches, and explorers made huge Brazil a Portuguese possession. Those prosperous years became known as the Glorious Age of Portugal.

But they were not so glorious for everyone. Many people, both in cities and rural areas, lived lives of utter poverty. Some families could barely afford enough food to keep themselves alive. They didn't even dream of the luxury of providing an education for their children.

I n 1495, a boy named John was born to a poor family in the town of Monte Mor il Nuovo. Although his parents couldn't give him many material things, they loved him dearly and taught him to love and serve God.

When John was eight, he disappeared from his home. Some say he was kidnapped. Others maintain that he went willingly with a wandering priest who had promised him adventures and riches. In any case, John soon found himself abandoned in a part of Spain called Castille. Friendless, penniless, and no doubt very frightened, he got a job helping a shepherd on a large estate. There he remained until he was twenty-two.

During all those years, John never tried to go home. He'd always been a dreamer, and his dreams had made him stubborn.

"Surely fortune will smile on me someday," he told himself. "I'll be a hero—a rich hero—and ride back to Monte Mor il Nuovo on a fine horse with bags of gold and heaps of jewels for my parents. Won't they be proud!"

With dreams of fame and riches on his mind, John jumped at the chance to join a group of soldiers who served Emperor Charles V. Europe offered plenty of wars in which such men could prove themselves.

"Any time now," thought John, "fame and riches finally will be mine!"

In those days, a soldier's life was rough-and-tumble, and John soon slipped into the ways of the men around him. He didn't want his comrades to think he was a sissy or a snob, so he put away all his religious training and lived as wild as his friends did.

When he was nearly forty years old, John took a long look at himself and was totally shaken by what he saw. "What a dreadful life I've lived!" he groaned. "How can God ever forgive me?" But then John had an idea. "The least I can do is to spend the rest of my days trying to make up for the past. Maybe I could care for the poorest of God's people." So John set off for Africa to help Christian slaves.

But when he reached Gibraltar, the Spanish port from which he would sail for Africa, his plans changed. He met a

Portuguese family who had lost all they owned and were
deeply in debt. John felt so sorry for them that he sold his
belongings, took a job, and began to support them. Then,
when they were on their feet again, he became a peddler,
wandering from city to city, selling religious books and
pictures.

John was such a good peddler that, by the time he was
forty-three, he opened his own shop in the large Spanish
city of Granada. One day, after work, he went to a church
service. The speaker's words touched him deeply, and an
immense, smothering feeling of guilt settled over John,
until is seemed as if he couldn't breathe.

"Mercy!" he cried. "Please, God, have mercy on me!"

He began to beat his breast and ran into the street,
screaming and tearing out his hair. The people who saw him
thought he was possessed by devils and threw sticks and
stones at him to drive the devils out. Finally, John crept
home, bruised and exhausted.

But the days that followed brought him no relief. Still
tormented by guilt, he gave away everything in his shop and
roamed the streets, crying and muttering to himself. Finally,
someone took him to an insane asylum.

Back then, asylums were terrible places. Keepers did
cruel and brutal things to try to cure their patients, and
patients often harmed one another. Fortunately, John was
not there long before the preacher whom he had heard
came to see him.

"You have gone too far, John," scolded the preacher.
"This isn't how God wants you to live. If you want to serve

God, stop your wailing and do something that will help others. You'll be helping yourself too."

John's keepers looked on and shook their heads. "That fellow won't listen to reason," muttered one. "He's just too far gone."

To their astonishment, John immediately became quiet. Furthermore, he stayed quiet. There were no more wild outbursts of tears and cries. And although he remained in the asylum a while longer, it was only because he wanted to help the other patients.

When he finally left, John was again ready to serve the poorest of God's people. He rented a house in Granada and turned it into a shelter for the sick and homeless. To earn money for the shelter, he sold wood in the marketplace or begged in the streets.

At first, some people criticized John. "Have you seen the sort of people he takes in?" they asked one another. "Wanderers, prostitutes, and who knows what other kinds of miserable scum!"

John didn't pay the least bit of attention to them. He now understood that not even wickedness could keep people from accepting God's love and forgiveness.

As time went by, more and more people realized what fine work John was doing. He was kind to his patients, but he was also wise. He found jobs for them when they recovered. He arranged for some to have long-term care in their homes. And he told all of them about God's great love for them.

Soon, wealthy men and women were donating money to

support John's shelter. Followers began to share his work, both in Granada and in other places throughout Europe. Then, word of John's wonderful accomplishments for the poor and homeless reached the archbishop of Granada, who gave him the name "John of God."

Ten years passed. Then, one day, a flood swept through Granada, washing away the wood John meant to sell and some other things he'd put aside for his shelter. Frantically he tried to save these belongings. But then he saw a man drowning and rushed to help him. By the time the man was saved and the flood had passed, John was thoroughly exhausted and sick.

"Take me to the shelter," he told some friends. "I'll get better there."

"No, John," said one of the women. "At the shelter, you'd just start working again. I want you to come to my house where you can get rest and proper care."

So John went to the woman's house—a mansion complete with chapel—and she sent for the best doctors and nurses. But it was too late. Although he was only fifty-five, John had worn himself out with work. On March 8, 1550, his nurses found John's lifeless body kneeling in the chapel, his face resting against a cross.

John was dead, but his work continued. Before long, his followers became known as the Brothers of St. John, and they worked in hospitals throughout Europe. John of God was canonized in 1690. He is the patron saint of nurses, hospitals, and the sick.

Teresa of Avila

It began with King Ferdinand and Queen Isabella in the late 1400s. Spain, they decreed, must be a purely Christian country. They would no longer have anything to do with people who did not share their beliefs.

The Spanish Inquisition was created to enforce this new law. Anyone suspected of lying about their Christian beliefs—or not believing as officials thought they should—could be questioned, tortured, and even put to death. As a result, people living in Spain spent a lot of time brooding over religion.

This terrible situation continued for hundreds of years and was a dark time in the life of the Spanish church. Even so, God managed to create light in the darkness.

awn had just broken on March 28, 1515, when Teresa de Ahumada was born at Avila, in central Spain. Her parents, Don Alonso, a knight, and Doña Beatriz, were wealthy and God-fearing people. Eleven brothers and sisters filled the family home, but young Teresa felt closest to her brother Rodrigo, who was four years older than she.

Like other Spanish children then, Teresa and Rodrigo heard a lot of talk about God. What impressed them most of all were the descriptions of heaven and the good things waiting there. Teresa, who always seemed to get her way, had an idea about how she and her brother could see heaven for themselves.

"Let's go off to a heathen land," she suggested one day, when she was seven and Rodrigo eleven. "When we get there, the heathens will cut off our heads and we'll be martyrs—people who died for their faith—and we will go straight to heaven."

Although he was older, Rodrigo trusted his sister completely, so off they went. Fortunately, they'd barely left town when they met an uncle who marched them back to their frantic mother.

Next, the two children decided to build themselves stone caves in the garden and live like poor hermits. But the caves kept tumbling down. Finally they gave up and searched for their adventures in books instead.

Full of daydreams and ideas from the books she read, Teresa found that the things she liked best were playing dress-up and spending hours in silly games with her cousins. Her fun would not last forever, though.

When Teresa was thirteen, her mother died. Suddenly life seemed much more complicated. She felt guilty about all the time she had wasted playing silly games and dressing up, and she often sulked. Don Alonso couldn't handle such moodiness, so he sent his young daughter off to a convent school, where she could be taught and raised by nuns. Teresa was quite happy in the school, though she had no desire to become a nun herself.

A serious illness brought her home again. While she was recuperating, an uncle read some religious books to her, and all at once Teresa felt afraid.

"If I had died from my illness," she told herself, "I would not have gone to heaven like a martyr. I'd have gone to hell! I have to change—to love God like the nuns at school. I had better force myself to want to *be* a nun. Wicked as I am, that will be the safest life for me."

Don Alonso did not approve, and he told her so. But the headstrong Teresa ignored her father and ran away to a Carmelite convent. Her father allowed her to stay. When she was twenty-one, Teresa became a Carmelite nun.

Her first twenty-five years in the convent were a mixture of pleasure and pain. The nuns there lived a far easier life than she could have guessed. It was nothing like the hermit games she and Rodrigo used to play. These nuns had plenty of time for visitors, gossip, and trips to town. Some even wore fancy jewelry with their plain habits. Teresa felt torn in two. She enjoyed the relaxed social life, but she also felt guilty about it.

During those years, Teresa also experienced shattering spiritual visions. Some of them seemed to come from God and others from the devil. Worse, she had no control over when the visions came. One might occur when she was with other people, freezing her in mid-sentence and turning her whole body rigid. Teresa was embarrassed and, often, terrified. When she consulted various priests for help, their conflicting advice only left her more confused.

Years of spiritual struggle and prayer finally caused Teresa to feel much closer to God. But she still was unhappy with the situation in her convent.

"You know," she said one day to a small group of nuns, "this is not the way we Carmelites should be serving God. Carmelites used to own nothing. They lived in small groups, not in huge convents like ours. They were poor, and they devoted their lives to meditation and prayer."

"Well," replied another nun, "why can't some of us start our own convent and live that way too?"

This simple suggestion was the light that finally showed Teresa what God wanted her to do with her life.

Within two years, Teresa and thirteen other nuns had moved to the new convent of St. Joseph in Avila. They slept on straw, ate no meat, rarely spoke, had no possessions, dressed in coarse brown robes, and spent their time in prayer and meditation. To the outside world, the most unusual thing about them was that they wore sandals instead of shoes. Because of this, Teresa and her nuns were called "barefoot" Carmelites. Teresa said the five years she lived in St. Joseph's Convent were the most peaceful years she'd ever known.

By 1567, though, she was out founding more convents, urging people to leave frivolous things behind and follow God completely. In the course of her life, Teresa started seventeen convents in all, but not without plenty of trouble. Some people disagreed with Teresa's changes, including Carmelites who wished to stay as they were. Once Teresa and her nuns were even brought before the Spanish Inquisition. The officials, however, found nothing wrong with them, and the "barefoot" Carmelites were allowed to flourish and grow.

Founding new convents meant travel, and Teresa felt a great dislike for journeys, especially long ones. She had to ride in covered wooden wagons over stony roads and through intense heat, bitter cold, flooded rivers, and endless swarms of insects. Her health was never good, and she often suffered during those trips. But just as often, it was her wonderful sense of fun and determination that kept her companions going.

That determination also helped Teresa get through all the controversy surrounding her new convents. She could—and did—match wits with anyone. One priest who argued against the new Carmelites groaned, "I would rather argue with all the theologians in creation than with that woman!"

In her books, which have become spiritual classics, Teresa tried to present as honest a picture of herself and her beliefs as she could. In her autobiography, she told of her life and her dramatic views on prayer. *The Way of Perfection* was written as a devotional guide for her nuns, and *Book of Foundations* told the story of the convents she had founded. *Interior Castle* described a spiritual journey toward God and brought light and hope to many people.

Teresa was sixty-seven and on yet another trip when she collapsed from her last illness. The sun had already set on October 4, 1582, when she died peacefully at one of her own convents.

Teresa of Avila was canonized in 1622 and, in 1970, together with Catherine of Siena, became one of the first two women to be given the title Doctor of the Church.

Martin de Porres

Tucked along the western hump of South America lies the country of Peru. The towering Andes mountains stretch from the north to the south of the country like a giant backbone, and waters of the Pacific Ocean lap its western shore.

Early in the 1500s, Inca Indians still ruled Peru and guarded its mountain treasures of silver and gold. But by 1538, Spanish invaders had conquered most of the country, plundered its wealth, and made the Indians their slaves. Eventually Lima, Peru's capital city, became the focus of Spain's vast South American holdings.

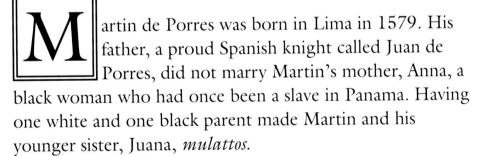

Martin de Porres was born in Lima in 1579. His father, a proud Spanish knight called Juan de Porres, did not marry Martin's mother, Anna, a black woman who had once been a slave in Panama. Having one white and one black parent made Martin and his younger sister, Juana, *mulattos.*

Since their father often went away and forgot about them for long periods of time, they were also poor. But Anna did her best to support the little family by washing clothes for other people. The children helped and, on the whole, they were happy.

Martin did have one habit that sometimes upset his mother: he liked to share whatever he had with others. If Anna gave him money to go to market and he met a sad-looking beggar on the way, chances were he'd give the money away. Or if he made it to market and bought some food, then met a hungry-looking dog on the way home, that would be the end of the food. Since the family had so little to start with, Anna's annoyance was understandable.

When Martin was twelve, Juan de Porres sent money to provide for his children's education. With this money, Anna apprenticed Martin to a local barber. In those days, barbers did everything from cutting hair to healing diseases and performing surgery. It soon became clear that Martin had a real gift for healing. Furthermore, he loved doing it.

Three years passed. Then, one night Martin heard God speaking to him.

"God wants me to serve him at the Monastery of the Holy Rosary," he later told his mother and Juana.

"You must do as he tells you," they replied. "We understand." After all, the monastery wasn't far away. They would still be able to see Martin from time to time.

So Martin trudged off to the Monastery of the Holy Rosary. He didn't want to become a priest, he told the monks there, or even one of the brothers who worked with the priests. He just wanted to be a servant and help out wherever he was needed.

"You are welcome to join us," said the prior, who was head of the monastery.

So Martin began a new life, cleaning and scrubbing,

mopping and polishing. He planted seeds, watered, and weeded. He made ointments, medicines, and teas from the plants he grew. Then, when his long day ended, he would often stay up all night praying to God, simply because he wanted to. Before long, others at the monastery saw that Martin was truly dependable and honest, so they gave him another job. The Spanish conquerors often donated large sums of money to the monasteries to use for poor people. Martin was to take charge of this money for Holy Rosary and make sure it was used fairly. For Martin, this was like a dream come true.

With the money, Martin started a hospital for homeless babies and an orphanage for older children. He handed out food, clothing, blankets, and medicine. He gave poor boys money so they could study to be priests and poor girls money so they could afford to get married or enter a convent. He cared for slaves, and he was even able to get prisoners released from jail.

Martin went on with his other work, too—especially his healing. As word of his healing skills spread, more and more sick people flocked to the monastery to see him. Some of the other monks began to grumble and complain.

"It's not healthy, all those sick folk hanging around," they muttered.

Martin knew that he would have to do something, so he talked to his sister, Juana. By this time, she was married and had her own home.

"May I treat my sick people at your house?" Martin asked her.

"Of course," said Juana.

"Then there are my sick dogs and cats," said Martin, who loved animals.

"We'll have a hospital for them, too," said Juana.

"Not all the dogs and cats are sick, though," said Martin. "Some just need homes."

"Then we'll add a shelter as well," said Juana. Obviously her heart was as big as her brother's.

Martin's love for animals wasn't limited to dogs and cats. According to one of the most popular legends about him, it included rats and mice as well. Martin felt sorry for the rodents because no one else seemed to like them. In fact, the other monks set traps for them.

"They're eating our clothes," complained one brother. "They're nothing but pests!"

"They're just hungry," said Martin. "I'll take care of it."

That evening he went to the room where the clothes were kept and found a whole troop of mice nibbling away.

"You'd better stop that, little brothers," Martin told them. "Otherwise you'll end up in a trap. Come with me instead. I promise you'll be fed."

Then, according to the legend, the mice let Martin put them all in a basket and carry them to a nearby field. From that day on, the mice stayed in the field and never again bothered the monks' clothes. Of course Martin fed them every day.

Other stories also grew up about Martin, especially about his healing powers. No matter who came to him—rich or poor, famous or unknown, black, brown, or white—Martin would do all he could to help.

Legend says that Martin healed the governor of Mexico, who had a sore throat and a high fever, by asking him to drink the "medicine" in a glass. The governor did and instantly felt well. But the "medicine" was just plain water. When a poor woman lay dying, Martin gave her an apple and told her to eat it. She recovered at once, too.

Martin didn't like people to talk about how wonderful he was, though. "I gave the governor some especially fine water," he would say. Or, "Well, it was a very good apple, you know."

Martin believed that it was God who was wonderful, and he was only God's servant. But, wonderful or not, the things Martin did have endeared him to countless people for hundreds of years. He loved God with all his big heart. He loved all the creatures that God made. And he showed that love by being a happy servant to all.

Martin died of a fever in 1639 at the age of sixty. In 1962, Pope John XXIII canonized him. Today Martin de Porres is known as the patron saint of social justice and harmony among all races.